Right Side Up Thinking in an Upside Down World

Right Side Up Thinking in an Upside Down World

Looking at the World through the Lens of Biblical Truth

Ron Gallagher

Lighthouse Bible Studies

Copyright © 2017 by Ron Gallagher

All rights reserved. No part of this publication may be reproduced, stored in a retrieval system, or transmitted in any form by any means without the prior written permission of the publisher, except for brief quotations of forty words or less.

Unless otherwise indicated, all Scripture references are taken from the New King James Version. Copyright © 1979, 1980, 1982 by Thomas Nelson, Inc. Used by permission. All rights reserved.

Scripture references marked KJV are taken from the Holy Bible, King James Version.

LEGO® is a trademark of the LEGO Group of companies which does not sponsor, authorize or endorse this book.

Published by Lighthouse Bible Studies, LLC,
PO Box 304, Buford, Georgia 30515

ISBN: 978-0-9994857-3-6

Dedicated ...

To the One Who Died for Me ~

This book, and anything else in my life with any possibility of enduring value, is predicated on the day when Jesus Christ and the Good News He came to offer became personal to me. The incredible mercy and grace bestowed in that initial meeting became the strength that sustained me and the hope that has inspired me in all the ups and downs in the years that followed. Whatever else this effort might represent, it represents Him first. Whatever enduring fruit it might bear is altogether His.

To the One Who Lives with Me ~

On a human level, this book is dedicated to my wife, Diane, who has made us a team, and who has dedicated herself to promoting, perfecting, protecting, and preserving the ministry that writing represents to us. She has declared war against fatigue, discouragement, empty distractions, and missed deadlines; and she conducts an ongoing search-and-destroy mission against any form of grammatical error or formatting faux pas. Without her, our website would not exist, or would be classified as a prime example of pathetic digital humor. She always downplays her contributions and points to the writing and messages conveyed as the only things that really matter. That mindset requires frequent reminders that even the most tantalizing meal would lose its appeal if you took it off the fine china and served it in a work boot. Neither the thousands of visits to our blog nor this book would exist without her.

To the Ones Who Walk with Me and Worship with Me ~

In spite of a lifetime of writing, my first serious challenge to pursue publishing came from a fellow church member who also happened to be an author. We met in a totally different context, but her passion for writing and encouraging others in the craft soon made its way into our conversations. She invited me to a writers' group she directed and declined to accept excuses for not attending. Her persistent prodding eventually led to the publication of my first article and a commitment to the path that eventually led here.

God brought another author into my life when I attended my first writers' conference. Our inadvertent meeting was not so inadvertent to God, as she became both a personal friend to Diane and me and a significant source of professional direction and support.

In addition to our Christian writer friends, our "church family" has been an endless source of encouragement and support. Their expressions of appreciation and testimonies of God's blessing have been a powerful defense on those days when I was tempted to question God's calling in this direction and whether writing was worth the effort.

With Deep Gratitude for His Matchless Grace,
Ron Gallagher

Contents

Dedication	v
Prologue: Unexpected Treasures in Unlikely Places	3

Part I Right Side Up Reflections on Selected Biblical Passages and Principles

Introduction: Glimpses of Life through the Lens of God's Truth	9
A Mighty Fortress, or Just a Blanket and Some Chairs?	12
Love Lessons	15
Armor: What Version Are You Wearing?	19
Wheels Up Forever!	22
No Opinion about Cats	27
Where's the Triumph?	30
The Golgotha Equation: An Exchange of Nothing	34

Part II Right Side Up Reactions to Holidays and Festive Events

Introduction: Lessons from Life in the Good Times	41
See How Much I Love You?	44
Lifeless Leftovers	48
Turning the Tables on Phoebe: A Mother's Day Reflection	51
A Living Memorial, or Just Another Pile of Rocks?	55
A Long Road to Freedom	59
A Zombie Nod to Halloween	63
Another Look at Re-Gifting	66
Christmas: Same Old Thing	69
Unwrapping a Christmas Mystery	72

Part III Right Side Up Responses to Cultural Conflicts and Political Issues

Introduction: Reactions to the Challenge of an Oppositional World	79
Wanna Hear Me Play My Smoke Detector?	81
BOLO for Goldilocks	85
It's Not a Battle Cruiser Anymore	90
Time to Clear the Air?	94
Is Freedom Just Another Word?	99
Crocheted Words and Verbal Doilies	103

Part IV Right Side Up Revelations from Life's Impromptu Lessons

Introduction: Random Reflections on Some of Life's Teachable Moments	109
Hope: $2.98, Plus Shipping & Handling	112
No Audition Necessary	116
Breaking Free from Two-Dimensional Christianity	120
Is God's Real Name "Harvey"?	124
Love Those Hoverboards	129
Dynamite: The Power Is in What It Does, Not in What It's Called	133
Ambushed at Walmart	136
For Mom: The Brightest Morning Ever	140
Broken but Priceless	144
Parable in the Park	147
Epilogue: The Last Scene	153
Meet the Author	157

Prologue: Unexpected Treasures in Unlikely Places

Prologue: Unexpected Treasures in Unlikely Places

We had not even settled on a solid working title when someone overheard a casual reference to my writing project and interjected a reasonable question. "What's the book about?" she asked. I should have had a nifty one or two sentence synopsis loaded and ready, but it caught me off guard, and all I had was an instant case of brain freeze.

In an attempt not to look as off-balance as I felt, I cocked my head to one side and wrinkled my forehead into what I hoped would suggest an attitude of thoughtful reflection, possibly like she had just asked whether our grasp of end-time prophecies might be jeopardized by Einstein's theory that space and time can be joined together to comprise a four-dimensional space-time fabric. In retrospect, the look was probably indistinguishable from the one I get when running past a dead skunk on the highway. In any case, her question may be yours as well, so I'll endeavor to provide a rationale and the hope attached to it.

God's Counter-Cultural View ~

My desire to embrace the challenge of understanding God's counter-cultural view of the world and life began to take shape early in my Christian life after hearing an evangelist, whose name I cannot recall, utter a statement in an almost offhanded manner. He didn't reinforce it with any special emphasis, perhaps because it was an idea already familiar to most of the congregation. Regardless, it was new to me, and I thought it was absolutely profound. This quote may not be verbatim, but the statement went something like this:

> God sees nothing in our life as "secular." From His point of view, everything about us and the world we live in is spiritual, or at the very least, has spiritual implications.

Perhaps it should have fallen into the category of common sense, but I had apparently not considered how all-encompassing God's involvement is in everyday life. I was intrigued by how functionally pragmatic He intended the Bible to be in regard to all that we do. That awareness reorganized my view of the world around me and reconstituted my basis for understanding the confusing and unpredictable vicissitudes of life.

The genius of God was astonishing to me. He provided the Scriptures as a *framework* wherein all that we know about life fits, and at the same time, He established a basis for maintaining a consistent, reliable, and authoritative point of view. That brings me to the rationale for our title.

Life Confronts Us with a Lot to Process ~

Life in this culture assails us with unprecedented rapidity. An endless stream of sights, sounds, data, and emotional stimuli overwhelms our senses every day, and our minds are continually confronted with fresh images to be processed. It's challenging enough to simply recognize and identify what some of those images are, but there are deeper and more vital questions to be considered. What do they mean? Where do they fit? What are we to do in response to them?

Experience alone doesn't always provide the answer to those questions. Exposure to images doesn't automatically explain what those images represent. Our optical apparatus will transmit an image to our brains whether or not we know what that image is or what it means. If we were to place a three-year-old in the captain's chair in a jetliner, his or her eyes would record and transmit the same set of images a qualified pilot would see. The child would observe the same gauges, dials, switches, levers, and knobs that adorn the console and could reach out to grab and manipulate them. The obvious difference is that the child would have no regard or concern for what might happen as a result of twisting the dials or flipping the switches. Exposure to life is unavoidable; authoritative explanations of life are not.

Unveiling the Rationale ~

In simple terms, my ongoing desire is to see life through the lens of God's eternal truth, to discern His activity in the real world we live in, and to share it with others. My hope is that God will use this book to stimulate a spiritual curiosity that will lead to life-changing discernment through a deepened relationship with Him. The absence of this discernment in the popular culture is painfully obvious.

God made the treasures of wisdom and understanding available, and He pleads with us to acquire them. But there's more involved than simply asking God to sovereignly dump them into our hearts and minds. The process, like the product itself, has a spiritual basis and cannot be had through human effort alone. No training program or academic certification can lay hold of them. Wisdom and understanding cannot be divorced from the God who designed them.

I invite each of you to join with me in that endless quest for discernment, wisdom, and understanding. *"Right Side Up Thinking"* is meant to direct us to the One who designed and developed the moral code by which all humanity will ultimately be judged, and because He is perfectly "righteous" (i.e., "right") about everything, keeping His viewpoint uppermost in our thinking is at least reasonable as we try to make sense of all that life throws at us. In a culture with a determined, pernicious practice of turning nearly every virtuous and Godly concept *"Upside Down,"* I see this book as one more effort at keeping the *"Right Side"—"Up."*

My prayer, and my great hope, is that this collection of vignettes, anecdotes, insights, and opinions might be an encouragement to all who read them. I am asking God to constantly stimulate our curiosity regarding what He is doing, not just in *the* world, but in *our* world. And finally, that God will grant each of us discernment that proves to be that very special key that unlocks a treasure that thieves can't steal and markets can't depreciate. May God bless you as we continue to serve Him together.

>In His Matchless Grace ...
>Ron Gallagher

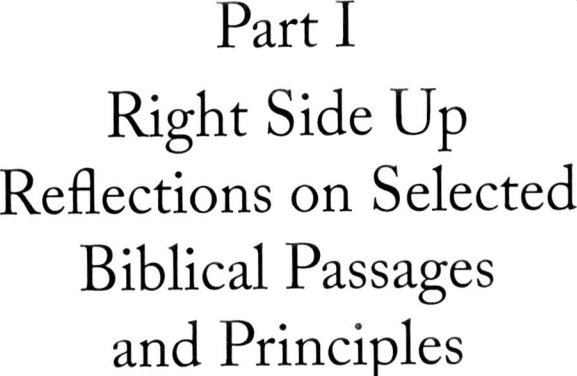

Part I
Right Side Up Reflections on Selected Biblical Passages and Principles

Introduction: Glimpses of Life through the Lens of God's Truth

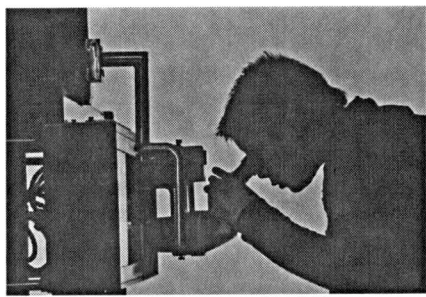

It was breathtaking. I felt like I had sneaked up to a small crack in a door and was secretly peering into a world that I never knew existed. Guys in 9th Grade Biology at that point hadn't been exposed to the marvel of nano-technology and high-resolution micro-imaging that are commonplace today, so when our teacher announced that we were going to be examining a drop of "pond water," I envisioned an attack of mid-afternoon boredom that could be lethal.

Instead, my little microscope lens revealed a tiny world that was teeming with life—creatures were everywhere in there. It was like prom night for weird little wiggly things. They were writhing, moving, twisting, and doing whatever it was that tiny creatures enjoy doing on prom night. It was fascinating, and life suddenly got a lot more interesting—although I did take a solemn vow never to go swimming in pond water again.

Solomon said that God has placed "eternity" in our hearts (Ecclesiastes 3:11). We are born with an embedded awareness that there is more to the world and life than we see on the surface, and we long to know things that exposure to the exterior alone cannot teach us. Jesus was God's response to that longing. In the same way that I could not possibly see the myriad forms of life thriving in our farm pond without a device to enhance my vision, neither could we see the profound truth He wanted us to know about life without Him. He made invisible things visible by lifting the veils that kept them hidden and in doing so, opened our eyes to the glory of God.

For instance, people have always wondered what heaven is really like and Jesus responded to that desire. But instead of producing a photograph or some kind of artwork that we could hold in our hands, He offered living panoramas for the mind that time can never fade. He often introduced them like this: *The kingdom of heaven is like ...* (Matthew 13:24, 31, 33, 44). Then He would proceed to point out some commonplace facet of life that His hearers could immediately recognize and use it to describe heavenly realities and perspectives capable of transforming lives and changing the world. Other times, He might unveil a glimpse of heaven with something as simple as a story. *A certain man ...* (Luke 10:30), for instance, might introduce an enlightening tale with unforgettable impact.

> The kingdom of heaven is like a mustard seed.
> Matthew 13:31

Unless and until we're able to align ourselves so that the Word of God is situated between us and the world we live and work in every day, our capacity for spiritual understanding will remain severely limited. Even though we might affirm a principle as true, the satisfying sense that we really "get it" comes from a grasp of how God intended it to fit in our lives. That's why Jesus made a practice of condensing expansive, eternal truth into a framework that was commonplace and easily understandable to those who heard Him.

God didn't become one of us in order to conduct academic exercises and deliver lectures on invisible beings and intangible principles in the sterilized atmosphere of a classroom. He came to take the Word of God out of the intellectual, religious museums where it is so often kept, and display it in the ordinary, everyday, understandable elements of life. That's where insights emerge that expose and explain spiritual realities that otherwise remain vague and confusing.

My family had several Bibles lying around in the house where I grew up, even though showing up in church was a random, unpredictable occurrence for us. Grandpa would read from one of them occasionally, but he never explained why he read it, and I never understood what any of it really meant. Bibles were just big books with lots of strange-sounding words in them. If anyone suggested that there was anything living in that book, I would have laughed out loud—but then again, I thought that the water in our pond was just water, too.

God doesn't obscure the deeper treasures of His Word to frustrate us. He does it so we can experience the delight of an unexpected glimpse into a world we didn't know was there, or the joy of hearing His "voice" rise above the drone of an everyday conversation. Or so we can feel the wonder of turning over another "leaf" in our daily routine and finding that special jewel He's been waiting for us to discover. My prayer is that this section will stimulate a greater desire in each of us to discover the unseen life God is waiting to show us in that Book.

A Mighty Fortress, or Just a Blanket and Some Chairs?

It didn't look much like a fort. What it did look like was a bedspread, a blanket, and some furniture. The apparatus was secured on one end by a dresser drawer and draped over the backs of two or three chairs to form a kind of crude tent, and a corner was pulled back to serve as a door. The boys had their army helmets on, their utility belts fastened around their waists, and their weapons in hand. I wanted to smile because the scene was so cute, but the look on their faces let me know that this was serious military business and no time for frivolity.

The enemy was doubtlessly lurking out there in the hallway somewhere, and everyone was in grave danger. This magnificent fort and their strategic genius constituted the last line of defense against whatever evil force was about to be launched against us. The fort was adequately supplied, of course. There was no shortage of Nerf gun ammunition, and the valiant warriors inside had enough snacks and bottled water to withstand an extended siege, even if it lasted until lunchtime. I couldn't help but feel safer knowing that such a fortress was in place.

Forts Are Not a New Idea ~

There's something primal, instinctive, and compelling, at least to guys, about the idea of building a fort. Whether we think of them in terms of ancient stone walls or the reinforced concrete bunkers of our own day, their objective has always been the same, to create a place of refuge, a safe place with an impenetrable barrier between a vulnerable people and the enemies they fear.

Fortresses are always in our thinking because in spite of our boasts of intellectual superiority and our continually expanding repository of information, we human beings can't seem to live in harmony with each other for very long anywhere. We are cursed with a selfish and contentious nature and prone to resort to violence, if necessary, to get what we want. Conflict stalks us continually. It may be as minor as another verbal assault on social media or somebody making obscene gestures at us from their car, as though a near collision that they had caused was somehow our fault, or it could even reach the level of an outright physical attack. The timing, circumstances, and impact may be unpredictable, but whether we're the perpetrator or the victim, conflict of some kind, at some point, will find us. It's almost oxymoronic that a people so conditioned to aggressive opposition and contentious interactions would, at the same time, harbor such a deep longing for peace and personal safety, but we do.

Our Fort Designs Have Built-In Flaws ~

Every new day comes with an awareness that there are enemies stalking our welfare on every side, and all of us long for a fortress where the things we fear can't get to us. The problem is that the fortresses we design always come with built-in flaws.

For instance, they aren't always available, and the fact that a fortress exists somewhere doesn't help at all if you can't get to it. And once you arrive, there's another problem. You have to find a way to get inside. That demands that your wonderfully fortified wall must have a gate, and gates can be problematic. Regardless of how tall and thick the walls are, if the gate can't be effectively secured, then your fortress only represents a minor delay to your attacker. In addition to that, there's the challenge of evolving weapons and tactics. If the enemy's arsenal is constantly evolving and the defenses in your fortress can't keep up, then you're in trouble.

God Has a Better Idea ~

No matter how we design our fortresses, they always fail eventually, because, like us, they all have flaws. That's why God invited us into a fortress sufficient for every circumstance—one we could never build on our own. David described it this way:

> *He who dwells in the secret place of the Most High shall abide under the shadow of the Almighty. I will say of the LORD,* **"He is my refuge and my fortress; My God, in Him I will trust."** (Psalm 91:1-2, emphasis mine)

The One who became our stronghold didn't look much like a fortress in the beginning. The attack against Him was devastating and left His torn and lifeless body hanging from the nails on a cross. A rock-hewn tomb claimed it for a while, but three days later, God shook the earth out of sleep and the body that walked out of that tomb was no longer weak and wounded. The One who absorbed and overcame every weapon the enemy had to use against Him now stands as an impenetrable fortress and invites us into Himself. No matter what form the threats and peace-robbing fears might take that haunt our days and nights, there's a secure place we can go that the enemy cannot reach.

The risen Lord who fought and won the final battle against our ultimate enemy will stand between us and the things we fear, and that longing for peace and security that drives us to build one flawed fortress after another can finally be fulfilled in Him. Anything short of that might as well be a blanket thrown over some chairs.

Love Lessons

Grandpa (my father figure for most of my early years) was very serious about teaching me what to avoid. The list began with snakes, bees, rabid animals, plundering Grandma's pantry, and making smart-aleck comments out loud. As I grew, my list expanded to embrace the usual roster of nightmarish nocturnal predators, which included ghosts other than Casper and anything with monster status, such as out-of-control body hair, weird teeth and claws, maniacal tendencies, or a penchant for eating people—especially kids. Then there was also that ill-tempered, antisocial carnivore that our neighbor, Mr. Easter, claimed was just a big dog. Oh, and of course—God.

Movies taught me about handling some of these threats to humanity, at least those with familiar cinematic exposure. Vampires, for instance, couldn't stand crucifixes, sunlight, or stakes through the heart. Wolfsbane, silver bullets, and staying out of the woods during full moons protected you from werewolves. Positive spells from good witches or curse-removing potions could neutralize ghosts that carried a grudge. Unfortunately, the movies offered no helpful guidance about dealing with the canine terrorist living at Mr. Easter's house—or God.

We weren't "church-going" people, so information about God was sketchy at best. Occasionally on Sunday afternoons, I would sit and listen as my grandpa read his Bible out loud. His favorite passages, as I learned later, were from the Old Testament prophets.

He didn't elaborate or explain anything, and some of the stuff he read about God sounded terrifying. For me, being a "God-fearing" kid was more a diagnosis than a compliment.

Santa's Scary Twin Brother?

To me, God sounded like Santa Claus' scary twin brother. Like Santa, God's headquarters was in a place normal people couldn't get to, and He was able to sneak in and out without a key. He was somehow looking at me all the time, just like Santa, and taking notes about all the stuff He saw me do. But instead of making cool toys to bring, God was busy thinking up ways to punish me for everything I did wrong. The worst I was likely to get from Santa was a lump of coal, but God could hit me with hellfire and brimstone (whatever that was).

Like God, Grandpa was big on rules, too. He had commandments and punishments for non-compliance which were (ostensibly) designed to make me better. Obedience was expected, and the only reward ever offered was relief from having dodged the painful consequences of failure. If teaching me to fear things was the underlying objective behind Grandpa's parenting strategy, mission accomplished.

What God Really Wants ~

The truth is, my grandpa never told me what his ultimate objective was and I never asked. He just made it clear that compliance with the rules was paramount. God makes compliance with the rules pretty important, too, but if we miss His objective in it, we miss the one thing He really wants us to learn. Maybe we should ask the simple question, "What does God really want from us?" His answer to that question is crystal clear.

You shall love the LORD your God with all your heart, with all your soul, and with all your strength (Deuteronomy 6:5). And the procedure designed to accomplish that objective is also clear: *And these words which I command you today shall be in your heart. You shall teach them diligently to your children* (Deut 6:6-7).

Let's ask another question. If love is God's primary desire, and if, as Jesus declared, that single concept encapsulates the collective impact intended in *all the Law and the prophets* (Matthew 22:40), what level of priority would we reasonably expect love to assume in His teaching plan for us, and conversely, in our teaching plans as parents?

Not as Simple as It Sounds ~

God's primary desire for us is that we learn to love—beginning with loving Him. That sounds simplistic, but the truth is that love the way God designed it isn't simple at all. It only sounds simple because we've reduced His infinitely glorious gift to a mockery of what He intended. The concept of "Love" has often been assaulted, raped, and abused in this culture until all that's left is a depleted, decimated shell. We retain the word, but that's about all. Love, like my understanding of monsters I had never seen, is all too often restricted to an isolated emotional genre, and merely the stuff of movies, legends, and fertile imaginations. We have little to teach about love because to our fallen nature, it is simply a mechanism for feeding an insatiable demand for selfish pleasure and a tool for manipulating others.

My grandpa wanted me to be safe, so he worked the idea of fear and avoidance of negative consequences into almost everything he taught me. He made rules and applied painful consequences for breaking them. We never had a session devoted to fear as an isolated topic—he just blended it into everything.

Finding Him—Finding Love—in Everything ~

God isn't interested in just teaching us how to pronounce a word that depicts some symbol of proffered affection. He wants us to know love like He wants us to know Him, and He wants us to find some aspect of it in everything. God wants us to know what love looks like, what it sounds like, what it feels like, what it acts like, who it touches, what it smells like, what it tastes like, what it does and doesn't do, how it wins, why it loses, what it fears, and where it leads. He wants us to know the toxic effects of its counterfeits, and the hopeless tragedy of its absence. Love is at the core of God's identity, and it is woven into everything He says and does.

> Love is at the core of God's identity, woven into everything He says and does.

A quest to find God's presence in every experience is essential training in teaching our kids that God's love lessons are everywhere. Every lesson God teaches us about life is a love lesson, and they don't always feel like the final scene in a Hallmark movie.

Armor: What Version Are You Wearing?

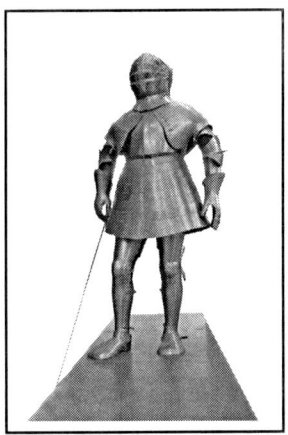

My image of a knight in shining armor got a little tarnished a few years ago. My wife and I had an opportunity to visit the Tower of London and a few other historical sites during a mission project we were helping with near London.

In a thinly veiled attempt to keep the men in the group from collapsing from boring artifact paralysis, the woman leading us mentioned that we were going to see the actual battle armor worn by King Henry VIII. Protracted exposure to such stimulating things as tapestries and dark paintings of people dressed in ways that could almost cause a rash just from looking at them, made the thought of seeing real battle armor downright thrilling. Most of us guys really like looking at stuff like that. Seeing what other guys wear while they're running around in a state of mass homicidal frenzy, trying their best to kill one another, is educational.

We eventually escaped the tapestries, and I could see the display case down the hallway that housed King Henry's armor. "Wow," I thought. "This is going to be great—real armor! This wasn't some cheap replica; this was what they actually wore into battle." I moved in close to get a good look, and then I had to do a double take. What a disappointment. I just never pictured knights in shining armor as being … well … short and fat. The metal figure reminded me of a friend who claimed he had a chronic condition that he referred to as Dunlop's disease. He said that his belly had "done lopped over his belt buckle so far, that he couldn't look down and see his feet without a mirror." King Henry had it, too.

Armor changes over time. The example I saw in London was the most advanced version available at the time, but now it is little more than an antique curiosity, fit only for display in a museum. To wear it for anything other than a theater prop or costume party would be ridiculous. What a difference a few years make. The metal had not deteriorated, and if we could find another person with the same body size, that old suit of armor would still work just as well as it did when Henry first put it on. The problem is that weapons and warfare have changed, and the armor had no capacity in itself to anticipate and adapt to the enemy's evolving arsenal, and its current construction is powerless against his weapons now.

The design of armor is always dictated by the enemy's capacity to inflict harm. Men don't devise armor to enhance their lounging comfort. They design it because human flesh is remarkably easy to penetrate, and because we have enemies. Bodies without protection are fragile, and vulnerable, thus the presence of armor and its ongoing evolution.

Physical wars have plagued humanity since the beginning, but there is a wholly different kind of warfare, the implications of which are even more significant. Paul has a couple of relevant comments on the subject of that kind of warfare and the armor necessary to defend against it.

He first reminds us that the warfare we're engaged in is distinct from the kind we normally think about, though it is no less real. He said that this warfare was not *after the flesh* (2 Corinthians 10:3 KJV) and that the weapons are not *carnal* (2 Cor 10:4 KJV), i.e., physical in nature. And further, the lethal threat that the enemy poses extends even into eternity, and is far more devastating than the loss of physical life. The different arena of our conflict dictates a difference in the nature of the weapons employed against us. That, in turn, requires a different approach regarding our defensive armor.

Paul admonishes us to *put on the whole armor of God* (Ephesians 6:11), and then proceeds to describe what those pieces are (Eph 6:14-18). Thinking about God's armor and looking at King Henry's provoked a thought or two.

> Unlike the suit of armor made for Henry VIII, God's armor fits every user perfectly.
>
> Unlike Henry's ponderous metal outfit, we won't need to shed God's armor because we get tired of carrying it around.
>
> Unlike Henry's armor, God's armor will never be outdated or need to be redesigned.
>
> Unlike Henry's armor, God's armor has no vulnerable cracks in it.
>
> Unlike Henry's enemies, ours will never have a device more powerful than God's protections.
>
> But just like Henry's armor, ours is very personal in nature and worthless if not applied, and like him, we are hopelessly vulnerable in battle without it.

And one final benefit—nobody will ever be able to look at our own version of God's armor and be able to tell whether we developed a case of the dreaded Dunlop's disease.

Wheels Up Forever!

My first airplane ride was in a 1940s vintage fabric-covered Piper Cub. I was all of fifteen years old, and though I had faced roller coasters, rickety carnival rides, all the *Wolfman* movies, and slow dancing with an actual girl, I never felt an adrenalin rush like the one pumping through me as we pushed the old yellow plane out of the barn. The anticipation by itself was almost overwhelming, but all of that excitement would soon be lost as my whole cardiovascular system was jerked into uncharted territory over and over for the next hour or so.

The cockpit felt small and cramped as I climbed in behind my new friend, who had now acquired sole possession of first place on my list of people I most wanted to be like. He looked over his shoulder and grinned as he settled into his place and waggled the joy stick between his knees. He flipped a toggle switch or two, felt the rudder pedals with his feet, and adjusted the throttle. Taking one more look around the outside terrain, he fixed his eyes on our intended path and engaged the starter.

Love at First Flight ~

The engine turned over slowly a few times and then sent vibrations through the frame and down my spine as it roared to life. We must have looked as surreal as I felt, sitting in an airplane in the middle of a southern Virginia cow pasture. Then we began to move. "My goodness," I thought as we bounced across the clumps of grass and other cow-pasture stuff, "I'm really going to fly."

The words had hardly formed in my mind when something magical happened. The world began to fall away beneath us, and the trees and fields and roads began transforming into a huge patchwork quilt that seemed to go on forever. It was love at first flight. My heart was gone, lost to this magic, and I knew that I would never fully get it back.

That was many flights ago, and even after hours of takeoffs and landings in my quest for a pilot's license while living in Alaska, I never lost the sense of wonder in that moment when the wheels leave the ground. It doesn't matter whether the wheels are underneath a Piper Super Cub lifting off a dirt runway at the edge of some Alaskan village, or the latest offering from Boeing or Airbus coming off the tarmac at a major international air hub—the feeling is the same.

The unique awareness that something special is happening has always accompanied liftoff for me. There's a kind of contest that unfolds in that process between two immutable laws. These laws collide with each other on the runway, and invariably, one must yield to the other as they vie for supremacy. The wonder of it has always intrigued me, and eventually led to a little ritual I find myself doing every time I fly. I'll explain in a moment, but first a word about the competing laws.

An Immutable Law that Says "No" ~

Regardless of an aircraft's design or capacity, there's a law that takes issue with the claim that it can fly. Whether it's a commercial airliner, a military plane, or a little homemade, one-man ultralight, a law says it can't leave the ground. It's simply the "law of gravity," and it's applied without discrimination or prejudice. An airliner worth millions gets no preferential treatment over a little Piper Cub two-seater.

"According to my law," gravity declares, "this plane will never leave the ground on its own." With no concern for the aircraft's size or shape, gravity's law steps up to declare without hesitation and with established authority, that it must remain firmly attached to the earth, held there by virtue of the undeniable weight of its construction and contents. Gravity's law is inarguable, and no aircraft, regardless of its technological complexity, has the capacity to dismiss the law or hide from its influence.

Another Law Is Introduced ~

Some years ago, a couple of curious brothers in Ohio began to investigate how and why birds are able to do what men and their cumbersome machines could not. They discovered that their wings were all shaped in a unique fashion, and this ingenious shape creates a never before recognized force when air flows over them. The force associated with that singular phenomenon came to be called "lift," and it gave rise to the creation of an entirely new set of principles, collectively referred to as the "law of aerodynamics."

This new "law" rises up to challenge the sentence imposed by the law of gravity. It is oppositional to the law of gravity, and distinctive in nature from it. The first law is fixed and requires nothing from us. Gravity simply "is." Its presence is pervasive, its force is constant, and it requires no effort on our part to maintain it. The law of aerodynamics, on the other hand, is focused, limited, and quite conditional. Its power is only available when specific demands are met and circumstances are put in place by those who desire to lay hold of its benefits.

Although gravity never ceases its determined effort to keep everything held to the ground, planes rely on the law of aerodynamics. They are equipped with wings whose shape was copied from the design God used when He created birds. As the plane picks up speed moving forward, the air flowing over the wing's unique shape begins to pull it upward. When the speed reaches a point where the force lifting upward on the wing exceeds the power of the weight pulling it down, something magical happens. The power of the law of aerodynamics takes over and the law of gravity can hold it down no longer. Gravity is overcome and has no more that it can do. It's "wheels up."

The Ritual ~

Every time we start down a runway, I focus on a single verse from Paul's epistle to the Romans, and just as the wheels leave the ground, I quote his words.

> *For the law of the Spirit of life in Christ Jesus*
> *has made me free from the law of sin and death.*
> Romans 8:2

That statement highlights another battle between two opposing laws, and the implications are far more critical than anything associated with gravity and aerodynamics. The "liftoff" God offers through His Son is much more incredible than leaving the ground in a man-made machine.

Different Laws—Eternal Implications ~

Just as gravity declares that a plane can't fly, the "law of sin and death" declares that I cannot rise above what I am, that I cannot live. That law declares that I will be eternally held down by the inescapable impact of my fallen sinful nature—trapped under the weight of innumerable transgressions. I have no power to remove that law, to evade its grasp, or to rise above its influence on my own.

Jesus did not seek to remove the "law of sin and death," but to overcome it. He didn't attack it or contradict it. Instead, He introduced another kind of force, one that would stand in diametric opposition to that law. Paul called it "the law of the Spirit of life."

Like the "law of aerodynamics," the overcoming force that Jesus offers is conditional. It is composed of two indispensable and irreplaceable elements—repentance from sin and faith in the sacrifice of Jesus Christ as payment for our transgressions. When those conditions are met, a force is unleashed that the law of sin and death has no power to overcome.

Wheels Up Forever ~

When lift overcomes gravity, a plane cannot help but fly. When we leave our sins behind and put our faith in Him, the "law of the Spirit of life in Christ Jesus" takes over, and the "law of sin and death" can hold us down no longer. At that point we cannot help but fly. The battle on the runway is over and it's "wheels up" forever.

No Opinion about Cats

Lots of folks seem to want to publicize parts of their profiles these days and kick-start our assessment of who they are, what they're about, and what kinds of categories we should put them in. Self-identity statements adorn cars, trucks, buildings, flags, T-shirts, and websites; and they get permanently tatooed into living tissue. We know things about people we don't even know—nor particularly want to know. I learned on my commute to work one morning that some guy has an opinion about cats that he considered to be worth declaring and perhaps defending. Interesting.

What Issue Would You Address?

I wonder, if we had to distill the most important thing we would want the world to know about us into something we could stick on the bumper of our car, what would it be? The things people choose to reveal about themselves are certainly intriguing. Many feel compelled to tell us what they do, what they believe, who they support, and what they refuse to tolerate. Some feel the need to warn us about dangers we might not realize, but they feel are important to know, like this one: "Meddle not in the affairs of dragons, for you are crunchy, and good with ketchup." Who knew?!! And, one of my favorites simply said, "Stop reading my bumper sticker, and go get one of your own." Okay, I did the first part. But if I wanted to do the second, it wouldn't display my opinion about cats. It would have to say something about God's forgiveness.

> How we handle forgiveness is connected to our personal experience with it.

Our ultimate handling of the subject of forgiveness, and especially God's command for us to forgive others, is inextricably connected to our personal experience with it—our own "forgiveness story," if you will. God was clear about that when He said through Paul that we are to forgive *one another, even as God in Christ forgave* [us] (Ephesians 4:32). Carrying out that directive requires that we know what it means to have been forgiven by Him. That makes our own experience and our own story a very important consideration when we're faced with the challenge of dispensing it to others.

A Story He Couldn't Stop Telling ~

I have a friend who, as he tells it, used to be a pretty good baseball player. I've heard him recount plays he made on the field as a shortstop—exciting tales of game-changing baseball acrobatics flow out of his mouth smoother than oil. Listening to him, you get the distinct sense that this is not the first time he's told that story. Truth is, some of his friends could tell those stories almost as well as he does. Contrast that with situations we've almost all encountered when someone was sort of backed into sharing their "God story," and they seemed awkward and uncomfortable, as though they might get it wrong.

If our personal forgiveness story has become only a vague, rarely visited, and nondescript piece of our religious timeline, then our forgiveness of others may reflect that. God doesn't see His forgiveness of us as a milestone we passed years ago. He meant it to be the atmosphere we live in every day, the story we can't stop telling. It is the wellspring out of which flows every hope we have for anything good in our lives right now. His forgiveness provides the only possibility of acceptance and a place in His house forever. It is our only connection to love that never fails, strength that never diminishes, and hope that never fades. It is the place where we can bring everything broken, no matter who broke it or how. It is the place where there's peace that can overrule and overcome every turmoil we create, and where joy lives in abject defiance of the circumstances that challenge it.

One Issue Dominates Everything ~

Forgiveness is the one thing that we could not lose and still retain anything of value. It is the one acquisition that carries with it the sum total of every treasure, and in such a form that no thief can steal, no government can confiscate, and no force can destroy. It connects us to the One without whom nothing remains but persistent frustration and emptiness, and eventual devastation and ruin. Forgiveness is a relentless and continuous exhibition of the heart of God toward us, and to live without that conscious awareness in this chaotic world is both tragic and unnecessary.

Every kind of philosophy and personal preference imaginable seems to find its way to somebody's bumper, trunk, license plate, tailgate, or rear window. On the back of my car, there's a little raised plastic thing that simply says, "Forgiven." If I have one thing to declare to the world about me, that is it. In the final analysis, it is the only thing about me that ever made anything else about me worth anything at all. Without it, there is only the painful, empty, and frustrating madness of life without purpose and meaning. If I had anything that I could bequeath to the world and everyone in it, it would be that. If I could choose an epitaph for my grave, it would be that. If I am ever moved to fall down and worship, it is to worship the One who looked at me in the broken and hopeless chaos of my life and offered me that. Forgiveness for me will never be "yesterday." It lives in every fleeting moment of "now." It is forever "today," and it is every "tomorrow" that I will ever be blessed to see.

Where's the Triumph?

The episode we've come to call "Palm Sunday" is celebrated by Christians around the world and begins what is popularly referred to as "Holy Week." It was an event full of profound implications, yet it involved no public exhibition of miraculous power, though there is little doubt that many in the crowd of pilgrims around Jesus on that day were hoping to see something like that. After all, the road they were traveling had brought them near the place where He had recently raised Lazarus from the grave, so anticipating another showy demonstration of divine authority would be reasonable as they approached Israel's religious capital at the holiest time of the Jewish year.

More than a Praise Word?

Their loud shouts of "Hosanna" were more than just a ritualized praise word. The term amounted to a collective desire blended into a passionate prayer and then condensed into a single word. It simply means "save now," and it was a perfectly appropriate request to offer because Israel was a conquered and occupied nation. They were chafing under the heavy burden of foreign occupation and longed to be free of Rome's oppressive and restrictive demands on their lives. They wanted a revived sense of national pride and spiritual well-being, and they wanted a resurgence of personal prosperity and security reminiscent of the glory days of Solomon.

Unlike the current conditions in America where the term "oppression" is likely to be invoked and weaponized in response to any situation that challenges someone's political, racial, or ideological preferences, the oppression in Israel was real, and the losses incurred were both personal and severe. Unlike those claiming oppression in our nation, the Jews of Jesus' day didn't have the option of rioting in the streets, burning chariots, and destroying buildings to make their point. Their only hope was that God would fulfill His prophesied promise and send a supernaturally-endowed leader, a new King, who would rise up and vanquish their enemies. People were saying that Jesus was the long-awaited "Anointed One."

But in spite of their shouts of praise, this physically unimpressive guy on a donkey may not have been as inspiring as they would have preferred. He didn't seem able or equipped to offer the kind of salvation they wanted, and if He was a king, He certainly didn't look like one.

A Perplexing Picture ~

Calling the episode "Palm Sunday" makes sense because of the reaction of the crowd in throwing palm branches ahead of Jesus' little procession, but we also refer to the event as Jesus' "Triumphal Entry," and that can seem perplexing. The picture we get from the text definitely shows excitement and enthusiastic anticipation, but Jesus didn't look like someone celebrating a major triumph.

For one thing, He was way underdressed for a triumphant procession. There's nothing to indicate that He even had a new outfit. As nearly as we can tell, He was clothed as He always was, in the common, ordinary garb of a rabbi from the poorer classes. He had no choreographed entourage to spice up His image, just the ragtag bunch of work-a-day men and women who followed Him around, listened to His teaching, and assisted Him in whatever way they could.

The Missing Pieces ~

If this was a triumph, it couldn't have been mistaken for a military one. In spite of any references that might have been made to identify Him as the Son of David, and thus the upcoming King of the Jews, the position apparently included no local military force, nor did He arrive attended by commanders or troops. Jesus had accomplished no heroic exploits on a battlefield that anyone else could have seen. He had engaged no human opponent in a physical struggle and had slain no human enemy.

He had no diplomatic triumph to claim or celebrate either. There was no aspect of problematic Jewish foreign policy over which Jesus emerged victorious as the Jews' premier statesman. He did not enter the debating halls to do verbal battle with Roman diplomats and attempt to win them over to His way of thinking. Neither did He confront the Greek philosophers in their academic halls and present His arguments in their arenas. He wasn't an official representative of any organization, agency, or government. He wasn't recognized as a leader of any currently recognized sect, party, or group. If this was a "triumphant" procession, it was definitely a peculiar one.

A Problem with Our Triumphant Heroes ~

Whether the crowd was a bit disappointed about any of that or not is pure conjecture but not outside the realm of possibility. After all, we want heroes to be larger than life, sporting a ride we can't afford, exuding a commanding presence we don't have, dressed in garments we could never wear, and displaying physical strength and intellectual genius totally beyond us. We want heroes who look like we want to be, not so much like what we are. The downside, in case you haven't noticed, is that our triumphant heroes riding on their prancing stallions don't invite us to join them, and certainly not to come home with them, or even to be like them. Quite the contrary. Instead, they can be smug and content in the awareness that they are not like us and that we cannot be like them.

Jesus didn't look like much by the world's standards of His day. But that's okay ... His triumph was not *in* this world's system or by this world's standard; it was *over* it. He did something the iconic "triumphant" stars and heroes the world produces refuse to do, and John described it with eloquent simplicity. *The Word became flesh and dwelt among us* (John 1:14a). Jesus didn't come to look down on us and be envied by us. He came to be one *of* us, and one *with* us.

Now, from His humble place on a simple donkey's back on His way to a cross, He calls to all of us in our ordinary clothes, oppressed by our flaws and failures, and bound in our frustrating weaknesses, to come follow Him, to be with Him, and to be like Him. He calls us to an eternal triumph over the sins that plague us and the death those sins demand. *Hosanna* is more than an ancient word from a bygone day; it's a prayer that He will answer for us ... here and now.

The Golgotha Equation: An Exchange of Nothing

Do you ever think about the idea of "nothing"? Men apparently struggled in the early days about how to deal with it, especially when it came to numbers. The philosophical reality of nothing had always existed, but people debated about different ways to understand and define it. Representing it in mathematical symbolism was a difficult challenge, and it was not until around the fifth century A.D. that the handy invention of the zero came along. Though the ubiquitous little circle eventually adapted itself to lots of roles, its primary purpose is to indicate the total absence of any content or value in the category to which it is applied.

I Learned about Nothing in High School ~

"Nothing" can be an intriguing subject. The first time I ever thought about it specifically was in a science class in high school. The subject of outer space had come up, and the teacher was about to have a spasm, gushing over how fascinating it was that outer space was comprised mostly of nothing—a total vacuum. She went on about how all that emptiness was why they called it "space," an immense expanse where for the most part, no substance of any kind existed.

It was interesting, but I didn't share her enthusiasm once I realized that the phenomenon was not that new to me anyway. A form of it had already existed in my head every time I was called on in math class. In any case, the concept of nothing plays a vital role in helping us understand and communicate certain realities of our world that would otherwise be hard to grasp or explain.

God Talks about Nothing ~

The idea of "nothing" is important to God, too, and He takes care to mention it repeatedly and in reference to different things. For instance, after describing His followers as "the salt of the earth," Jesus uses the term to point out what the salt would be worth if it lost its primary quality, saltiness. He said it would be, *good for nothing* (Matthew 5:13).

In explaining His metaphor of a vine and its branches, He said that if a branch is not secured in the vine, it is powerless to produce any fruit, and then declared to them, *Without Me you can do nothing* (John 15:5). When defending the simplicity of the gospel message, Paul reminded the Corinthians of God's promise that He would *destroy the wisdom of the wise, and bring to nothing the understanding of the prudent* (1 Corinthians 1:19).

A Confluence at the Cross ~

A personal confrontation with the stark emptiness of "nothing" can be a sobering experience, depending on where we stand in relationship to it, and it is never more sobering than when that concept converges from different directions at the cross of Jesus Christ.

The idea of "nothing" first emerges shortly after Jesus had just reminded His disciples again of His imminent departure. *I will no longer talk much with you,* Jesus said, *for the ruler of this world is coming, and he has nothing in Me* (John 14:30). Satan was coming after the Son of God with everything he had, intent on finding or creating anything that he could claim as his own. Jesus declared that the devil's quest was fruitless and futile, and that he would find "nothing" in Him that was less than righteous. No other human being in history had been, or ever would be, able to say that truthfully.

At the trial, after both Pilate and Herod had examined Jesus, Pilate announced, *I find no fault in Him* (John 19:6), and declared finally that, *nothing deserving of death has been done by Him* (Luke 23:15). Satan unleashed every force at his disposal in search of any hint of sin and found ... nothing.

When we're the ones on trial and that kind of examination is focused on us, the results are quite different. Since Adam's fall, we who were created to reflect the image of God are found to be universally drawn instead toward the image of the serpent. Selfishness, disobedience, dishonesty, lust, rebellion, deceit, stubbornness, and violence are behaviors no one has to teach us. God declared that apart from Christ, in the entire race, *there is none righteous, no, not one* (Romans 3:10).

Inspired by the Spirit of God, Paul confessed himself as an example, *For I know that in me (that is, in my flesh) nothing good dwells* (Rom 7:18). Apart from God's direct intervention and the Holy Spirit's control, there is "nothing" in us that is good or acceptable to our holy and righteous Creator.

If we heard someone suggest that the cross of Jesus Christ was all about "nothing," we would very likely be shocked and declare it blasphemous. But what if we saw Calvary as the most profound and meaningful confluence of the concept of "nothing" that the world has ever known?

On Jesus' side of the "Golgotha equation," the "nothing" quantity emerged on every occasion when Lucifer came to Him looking for some flaw, some defect, some momentary lapse, any failure on His part to physically embody the perfect righteousness of God. The devil used every tool, applied every test, unleashed every temptation, and seized every opportunity to somehow inject into Jesus his own satanic DNA, and in every case, he came away with "nothing."

Our side of the equation involved a different kind of search, but with the same "nothing" result. God examined us in our natural state looking for anything that reflected His likeness, anything about us that escaped being tainted by sin, anything pure, anything good, anything just, anything righteous, anything holy, and anything in us that looked like the love He bestowed on us. He examined us all and found "nothing."

The Equation Comes Together ~

The Son of God brought His glorious "nothing" to that mockery of a trial. He stood there bearing nothing worthy of death and looked out at a crowd having nothing worthy of life and said, I'll trade you.

With a love that we cannot understand, He offered His life, empty of sin, and took on Himself the full weight of consequences deserved by lives that were empty of righteousness. The condemnation that our kind of "nothing" demanded was poured out on Him, and now He freely offers us the glory that His kind of "nothing" achieved.

Oh … And in case anyone ever asks what we did to earn such a gift, here's the answer … nothing.

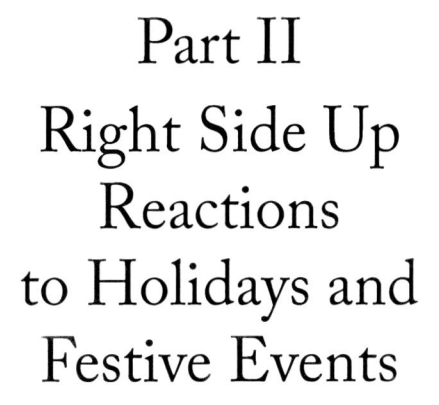

Part II
Right Side Up Reactions to Holidays and Festive Events
~

Introduction: Lessons from Life in the Good Times

God is the original inventor of the holiday. Throughout history, He has been an avid proponent of setting apart certain days and designing festivals and celebrations to remember and honor significant events. The scope of the potential impact attached to them is impressive. For instance, holidays have the capacity to reach back into the past as far as necessary to remember God's direct involvement and to experience it again in retelling the stories associated with it.

Beyond that, holidays bring with them real-time, hands-on opportunities to engage with God, because He never intends to leave us to celebrate alone. He prefers to show up and bring His unique brand of joy and to create an atmosphere of positive optimism so that His presence is characterized by things that are uplifting and encouraging. He is always teaching, and He prefers to have His lessons absorbed in the context of blessing and provision, rather than judgment, grief, and loss. Holidays are one of His favorite ways of taking us to school without having it feel like that's what He's doing.

Then there's the anticipation that gets built into our holiday celebrations. They become traditions, and traditions are preludes for the sequel that we expect to be unveiled next year. Every remembrance of God's faithful provision in the past and every acknowledgement of His inspirational impact in the moment, carry an expectation that He will continue to exhibit the same loving care for us in the future. Whether we articulate that expectation or not, it infuses itself in our minds and hearts and becomes a part of what we are actually celebrating.

And then there are those special times when we can almost feel the power of God's presence in the celebrations of His people just from reading accounts like this one.

> *So the children of Israel who were present at Jerusalem kept the Feast of Unleavened Bread seven days with great gladness; and the Levites and the priests praised the LORD day by day, singing to the LORD, accompanied by loud instruments. And Hezekiah gave encouragement to all the Levites who taught the good knowledge of the LORD; and they ate throughout the feast seven days, offering peace offerings and making confession to the LORD God of their fathers.*
>
> *Then the whole assembly agreed to keep the feast another seven days, and they kept it another seven days with gladness. For Hezekiah king of Judah gave to the assembly a thousand bulls and seven thousand sheep, and the leaders gave to the assembly a thousand bulls and ten thousand sheep; and a great number of priests sanctified themselves.*
>
> *The whole assembly of Judah rejoiced, also the priests and Levites, all the assembly that came from Israel, the sojourners who came from the land of Israel, and those who dwelt in Judah. So there was great joy in Jerusalem, for since the time of Solomon the son of David, king of Israel, there had been nothing like this in Jerusalem. Then the priests, the Levites, arose and blessed the people, and their voice was heard; and their prayer came up to His holy dwelling place, to heaven.* (2 Chronicles 30:21-27)

Whether it's Christmas, Easter, Thanksgiving, or one of our not-so-spiritual holidays, some of our most cherished lessons about life, faith, love, family, hope, and the God who ordained all of it are learned in the midst of them. Those lessons cry out to be preserved and shared, and they live on in the holiday stories we share with each other. They have the capacity not only to strengthen our human connections, but the spiritual ones they were designed to reflect as well.

We serve a divine Lover of holidays, festivals, and special occasions; and my prayer is that everyone who explores this section will be encouraged to invite Him into every special event and look for Him in every celebration. He is, after all, the God who said that He would be "with" us, and He delights to engage us in those days that we have sanctified in one way or another. When we seek His presence in the level of our mundane routines, we may find

> Look for God in every celebration.

that His involvement adds more than an extra dose of joy to our feasting. There may be *eternal* benefits we didn't expect, and that makes our future celebrations even richer.

See How Much I Love You?

As another Valentine's Day was looming on my calendar's horizon, I was confronted with a commercial for yet another surefire way to promote and enhance our romantic relationships. It was just what every couple needs—a huge stuffed bear. When I say "huge," I mean it was at least as tall as an average guy and sported a waistline about twice the girth of the dude carrying it. Watching the two of them trying to squeeze through the door evoked visions of a classic *Three Stooges* scene.

Once inside, the hopeful bearer of the bear proceeded to present it to the object of his affection with a mixture of pride and humble gallantry worthy of knighthood in any generation. She looked at the huge floppy thing as though it was a trophy he earned for unhorsing the evil black knight and thereby saving the entire kingdom—a selfless and heroic deed no doubt fueled by his passion for her and all things righteous and noble and done while flying her perfumed hankie from the little pointy thing on top of his helmet.

A YouTube-Worthy Tutorial ~

Her widened eyes revealed a combination of excitement mingled with stunned disbelief. Then her face took on a dreamy look as she stared at the bear and pondered what all the love-starved women watching would want to know in that situation. "How on earth did this heretofore romance-challenged dud of a lover ever manage to dream up something as wonderful and emotionally stimulating as this enormous dust bunny on steroids?" Whereupon her demeanor morphed into something clearly meant to suggest activities that shouldn't be shown on family friendly TV. In any case, the production was intended to convince the viewers that this was a YouTube-worthy tutorial on how to create an unforgettably romantic relational milestone.

I can imagine my wife's eyes if I came home with a thing like that. It would be akin to me coming home with an announcement that I felt led of the Lord to breed skunks as a ministry. The bear was so huge it needed either its own piece of furniture to flop on or a separate closet to hide it in—or both. Anybody taking that thing to bed had better be planning to sleep alone, because there would be no place left for anybody else.

An Alternative Perspective ~

Come to think of it, maybe that's the real attraction women have for these bears. Maybe the adrenalin rush they get when they see the insensitive redneck they're attached to dragging one of these things through the door doesn't have its roots in romance at all. Maybe it comes from the realization that this mass of foam rubber and fuzz could be just the leverage needed to finally pry him off her side of the bed—or even into his own bed—and allow her to get some decent rest for a change. After all, huge stuffed bears don't snore or make other unintelligible noises in the night, and they don't have breath that could strip varnish off antique furniture. A stuffed bear won't drool all over the pillow, and it won't be thrashing around half the night like an outnumbered Ninja warrior fighting for his life. Hmmm ... I think I'm beginning to see the real magic in these stuffed bears now. It's passion, alright, but not the romantic kind. It's the passionate desire for an uninterrupted night's sleep.

Okay, I agree with those of you thinking that exploring the motives and methods involved in the trafficking of stuffed animals is a bit lacking in spiritual relevance. But commercials like the one just mentioned do give us an interesting glimpse at the kinds of bizarre things we do (especially in February) in an effort to say, "I love you." We go to ridiculous lengths every year to create and market quirky new ways to demonstrate whatever series of emotional convulsions we decide to call "love." That tendency at least grants us a warrant to indulge in a spiritual observation or two, because devising ways to express love is an endeavor near to the heart of God.

That being said, the whole Valentine's Day phenomenon is a recurrent reminder that the chasm that separates our customs associated with romance and God's approach to expressing love is difficult, if not impossible, to exaggerate. It's daunting to compare the superficial trinkets we often present to one another as validation of our undying love and devotion versus the kinds of things God chooses in His effort to do the same thing. It would seem reasonable to expect that the things we offer as expressions of the nature and quality of the love we profess ought to be consistent with the nature and quality of the love itself. If we declare a love whose strength and value overshadow everything else in our lives, then to the best of our ability, things chosen to express it should reflect that. To do less would seem to demean or redefine the love we claim to have, or worse, expose our declarations as being altogether disingenuous.

Divine Expressions with Real Connections ~

Consider a couple of love expressions that the Lord Himself found impressive. The first event is customarily treated more as a faith issue than a love issue, but I believe that love and faith are interconnected concepts, just as love and trust are. As Jesus stood observing the parade of those making offerings at the temple, the offering of a poor widow caught His attention. Her offering was of such little value that most would have thought it irrelevant, if not insulting. Jesus did not. We would probably paraphrase His initial reaction like this, "Hey, did you guys see that!" Then He made this comment:

> *Assuredly, I say to you that this poor widow has put in more than all those who have given to the treasury; for they all put in out of their abundance, but she out of her poverty put in all that she had, her whole livelihood.* (Mark 12:43-44)

In Jesus' mind, that woman's expression of her love, devotion, and trust in God surpassed anything offered by all those rich guys who came by. She had no possessions to offer worthy of the love she felt, so she simply gave everything she had—what an incredible expression.

Then there's the example of a broken woman whose redeemed heart became a fountain for a love that she didn't know how to express (Luke 7:36-38). As she knelt at Jesus' feet, the love that filled her heart found its way to her eyes and dropped onto the feet of the One who would take her sinful and wasted life, transform her, and treat her as though it never happened. Her expression of love was criticized by those who watched as she kissed His feet and wiped them with her hair. It was a simple act and not worth much in the marketplace of the culture, but Jesus found it perfectly suited to the love that prompted it.

Love is in the air around Valentine's Day, or so we're led to think. Perhaps what's in the air needs a fresh look and an honest comparison with what's really in our heart. If all we can come up with to express our undying love is some commercialized superficial trinket, could it be that what we have inside is not such a treasure either? After all, aren't we glad that Jesus didn't show up with a giant stuffed animal for each of us saying, "Here—see how much I love you?"

Lifeless Leftovers

It's intriguing how God often avoids details that many would have chosen to include, and inserts ones that seem to be oddly incongruent with their surroundings. For instance, He restricted most of the horrific details involved with Jesus' crucifixion to the private screening room of our imagination. Avoiding gory descriptions of physical torture, He chose instead to disrupt our focus and include the following:

> *Then the soldiers, when they had crucified Jesus, took His garments and made four parts, to each soldier a part, and also the tunic. Now the tunic was without seam, woven from the top in one piece. They said therefore among themselves, "Let us not tear it, but cast lots for it, whose it shall be," that the Scripture might be fulfilled which says: "They divided My garments among them, and for My clothing they cast lots." Therefore the soldiers did these things.* (John 19:23-24)

Attention is moved unexpectedly to Jesus' garments, the only physical remnants left of His ministry. It was a meager legacy as far as material things are concerned, but one that was nonetheless a very real and personal part of His life. They accompanied Him everywhere. They adapted to His frame, moved as He moved, went where He went, and stood where He stood. Perhaps He was wearing that robe when He called Lazarus back to life, or when He cursed the fig tree, or when He cast those demons out of Mary Magdalene. But once taken from Him, they were just empty cloth—no power resided in them, no life, no hope, no miracles, just the dead leftovers of a man whose life would change the world forever.

The Roman soldiers laid claim to His clothes even while their owner was still alive, which was common practice at the time. One of the rewards offered to those who engaged in the grisly business of torturing people to death was the right to claim the garments of the victims, along with whatever else they might have had with them. In Jesus' case, four soldiers wanted the garment, and tearing it apart to divide it didn't make sense, so they decided to cast lots to see who would win it. The hardened soldiers apparently expressed no hesitation in conducting their selfish and heartless game in the shadow of the very cross that would take His sinless life in exchange for their own. In the midst of His agony, they saw value only in what was His, but not in Him.

The soldiers weren't the last ones to see value in Jesus' personal property. Centuries later, Hollywood began to smell a possibility of profit as well, and at least one movie was produced about Jesus' robe back in the 1950s. The film was called, appropriately enough, *The Robe*. The fictional account purported to follow the path the robe took after the crucifixion, and the impact it had on those who possessed it. The writers attributed a mystical power to the garment that miraculously transformed the lives of those who had contact with it.

More recently, another story was conjured up about an item that Jesus used at least once, though no evidence exists that He ever actually owned it. That story revolved around the cup that He used in His final Passover meal with His disciples, and was bequeathed by Hollywood with even more magical properties than those it had granted to His robe in the earlier movie. The cup, which somewhere in history was dubbed the "Holy Grail" (much more impressive than just calling it a cup, I guess), was endued in this film with the power to transmit eternal life to whoever drank from it. Finding the magical grail, in true Hollywood fashion, demanded subjection to an adrenalin-pumping stream of devious international intrigue, random gunplay, life-threatening personal and vehicular acrobatics, manipulative romantic expressions (void of any real relationship, of course), and assorted examples of nefarious Nazi mayhem. In spite of the fact that the good guys prevailed and the bad guys (and gal) got their just deserts in the end, no one managed to acquire eternal life, not even pretend eternal life.

Such is Hollywood's take on stuff left behind by Jesus, and as shocked as I am to hear myself say it out loud, I agree with them—nothing of any eternal spiritual value is to be gained by anything material that the Son of God might have left behind or had contact with. The power is in Him, not in the stuff.

As comments like, "Yeah, we already knew that" begin to form, I have a question. Why, if we are so clever as to have figured that out already, do we exhibit such a tendency to attach more value to things associated with Him, than Him? Exhibitions of devotion and allegiance to the buildings that we call churches seem more prevalent than personal submission to the One who founded it. We seem to be more comfortable in venerating the rituals we have declared to be holy than in striving for personal holiness itself, and more ready to attach great value to the book in which His Words are written than to embrace and apply the meaning of those words in our lives.

The woman who received healing because she touched the hem of His robe didn't get it from the material she touched with her hand. Jesus wasn't wearing a therapeutic jacket, and He did not remark to His disciples that He felt some power leak out of His robe. Transforming power never comes through handling what touches Him, but in touching Him, and personal faith is the only effective means ever approved by which to do that. Gambling over lifeless leftovers while ignoring the One on the cross didn't end at Calvary, and as it was then, that game allows no winners.

Turning the Tables on Phoebe: A Mother's Day Reflection

Some parts of the Word of God are intellectually gripping the moment we read them. They sound like what we think inspired Scriptures ought to sound like, and we recognize their unique nature without some impassioned orator prodding us about their deep theological implications. When we read a statement like this, for instance: *And the Word became flesh and dwelt among us* ... (John 1:14a), we don't need a study Bible with a footnote in bold type to alert us that those are important words. People with keen spiritual sensitivities like us, and folks with an IQ score greater than their shoe size, notice right away that these words are significant because they're saying things outside the normal range of ideas.

Unfortunately, though, not every comment in the Word of God is as quick to set off our spiritual content alarm and have us reaching for a highlighter. Some verses in the "Book of Books" sound pretty commonplace and ordinary, like something we might have said or written ourselves. We wonder why some of those passages were included at all, and what, if anything, we're supposed to do about them. I ran across one of them again recently, and it claimed squatter's rights in my head and heart for a while.

Disturbingly Ordinary ~

Here's the passage:

> *I commend to you Phoebe our sister, who is a servant of the church in Cenchrea, that you may receive her in the Lord in a manner worthy of the saints, and assist her in whatever business she has need of you; for indeed she has been a helper of many and of myself also.* (Romans 16:1-2)

OK, so Paul is saying some nice things about Phoebe. I get it. But what's so special about that? Why wouldn't he? After all, once Jesus got him over being a brutal religious tyrant, Paul turned out to be a really sensitive, considerate guy. Now, instead of throwing Phoebe in jail, or maybe having her stoned to death, he's saying nice things about her. But maybe that's not the whole point.

When these words were written, Paul had just penned the bulk of one of the most profound spiritual documents that ever had been, or ever would be, written. The book of Romans has been called a "manifesto of the Christian faith," and represents a composite of New Testament doctrine that is unparalleled. Now Paul was adding a final, concluding section, and though it sounds very different from the fifteen chapters that precede it, it is as inspired as the rest of it. No profound doctrinal expositions unfold in this section, and there's not much that seems to just leap off the page at us. It's mainly a collection of personal notes to folks whose names sound really unfamiliar. I've never met anybody named Amplias, for instance, or Tryphosa, and Philologus sounds more like a medical term than somebody to share a cup of coffee with. So, what does God want us to do in response to these comments?

Turning the Tables?

Paul's simple remark about Phoebe wouldn't let me alone. She was obviously important to him, though we aren't given any details about her specific contributions, just her name, and that her helping efforts benefited him and lots of other folks as well. Paul pointed her out to everyone who would read his inspired treatise and as much as said, "Accept [receive/embrace/welcome] her." Then he suggested that the tables be turned. "Whatever she's doing," he said, "help her." It was time that she started to get back some of what she had been handing out to others, so he said, "If she needs anything for whatever she's doing, see that she gets it."

> Receive
> Embrace
> Welcome
> Help

Phoebe's role was important enough to be inscribed and stand alongside all of Paul's inspired insights and doctrinal expositions. All who might be praising God for his ministry and the work he was doing would hear him say, "I didn't do this—couldn't have done this—by myself."

Vital, but Not Ostentatious ~

Phoebe's work was vital, but not ostentatious. She was a behind-the-scenes person, left unknown or overlooked by most. She wasn't in the limelight, didn't write lofty epistles, didn't preach, or expound at length on doctrinal issues. She didn't plant churches. She didn't engage in theological debates, or publicly challenge those in power. She just helped. Probably few even knew what that really meant, but those she helped did. Maybe no one but Paul and God knew how many times her help made the difference in whether his task at the moment succeeded or failed. Regardless, neither God nor Paul were content to leave this quiet helper unacknowledged.

I've thought a lot about Phoebe recently, because I live with her. Well … OK, someone like her. They hate to hear themselves mentioned, but God made it clear that He wants the Phoebes in our lives pointed out, and it's time to comply. My version of Phoebe had a birthday not long ago, so it's a good time for me to step up and be obedient, although it's strange to feel so good about doing something I know she's going to hate.

More than a Character Trait ~

If there are "Phoebe genes," my wife got a major crop of them, because like Paul's Phoebe, helping is who she is. She never engages in self-promotion, will find last place in any line, and with no hint of hesitation, will happily sacrifice her portion of anything to anyone around who seems not to have one. She avoids spotlights, stages, platforms, and podiums. She doesn't teach, though she could. She doesn't make speeches, but not because she has nothing interesting to say. She takes nothing that isn't hers except the burdens and struggles of those around her. She loves much louder and more often with her hands than her words. Like Paul's Phoebe, mine has faults, or so she claims, but like Paul, I have no interest in wasting my time trying to figure out what they are. Her name may not appear on things I publish, lessons I teach, or messages I deliver, but nothing I do is minus her touch, and her help.

Let's make our next Mother's Day a time to honor all the "Phoebes" in our lives with more than just a Hallmark card sentiment. Let's turn the tables and help them for a change, and declare to all who know us that we'd be a much poorer version of "us" without "her."

A Living Memorial, or Just Another Pile of Rocks?

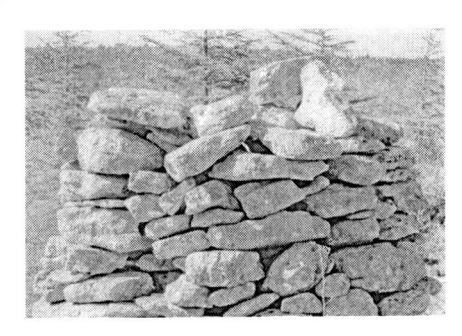

No summer day, not even Virginia's notorious "dog days" of August, ever intimidated my grandpa into wearing a short-sleeved shirt. Long-sleeved shirts were as much a trademark as his hat and that little half-smile he held in reserve for those rare incidents that were particularly hilarious. His tendency toward understatement and concealing things that didn't need to be exposed was a characteristic that extended to every part of his life.

Not the Usual Kind of Picture ~

One of the very few physical things I inherited from my grandpa, who was in every practical way a father to me in my early years, was a picture. It wasn't one of those pictures you often see of a guy from that era where he's standing there rigid as a board with a deadpan, half-angry look, like maybe his wife tricked him into wearing his "funeral suit" and he discovered too late that nobody had really died.

My picture was encased in a black wooden frame about eighteen inches long and eight inches high—the biggest, longest photograph I had ever seen as a kid. The 387th Infantry Regiment of the US Army was standing at attention, shoulder to shoulder, and arranged on a set of bleachers so that everyone's face would be visible to the camera. Their role as defenders of America was officially memorialized on that day, September 5, 1918, and my grandpa was on the second row. One click of a shutter captured that brief moment of his life nearly a hundred years ago, and now I have it. The sad thing is that I only have the memorial, not the memory. The photographic monument was passed along, but I was not allowed to inherit the meaning.

Something's Missing ~

That picture was taken near the end of World War I, a global conflict that saw the death of some 9,000,000 combatants and 7,000,000 civilians. Sadly, I learned those facts about "The Great War" from history books, not from my grandpa. Like all monuments, my picture was just a lifeless symbol with no capacity to add anything or transmit anything beyond its presence.

Monuments need more than that—they need memories. Monuments are dead things. Memories live. Monuments don't experience life. People with memories do. Monuments don't think, can't feel, and are powerless to move on their own. Monuments neither love nor hate. Monuments can only assume their position and wait until some living person comes along to explain them.

A Peculiar Command with a Memorable Lesson ~

In bringing His people into the Promised Land, God highlighted their predicament when He issued this unusual command:

> *Cross over before the ark of the LORD your God into the midst of the Jordan, and each one of you take up a stone on his shoulder, according to the number of the tribes of the children of Israel, that this may be a sign among you when your children ask in time to come, saying, "What do these stones mean to you?" Then you shall answer them ... And these stones shall be for a memorial to the children of Israel forever.* (Joshua 4:5-7)

The rocks they picked up were just rocks, different shapes and sizes, and maybe some variation in color, but just rocks. They weren't polished rocks, or engraved rocks, or rocks containing precious metals or valuable gemstones. They were just plain old, nondescript "bottom of the river" rocks that happened to be exposed because of the miraculous events that occurred in their presence—events to which, by the way, they contributed nothing.

We don't know what any individual rock looked like or what the finished monument looked like when they were all stacked up. Their only significance was that they were in the presence of a supernatural event. They didn't observe anything, feel anything, or remember anything. They were just a lifeless part of the landscape, helpless to experience or explain anything about the astounding power of God.

God's intention was clear. His people were expected to explain to their children why those stones were there and what they meant. The expectation was that parents would bring their kids to that place, and in the presence of that simple monument, would tell them the story of where the rocks came from, and how God made them accessible. The rocks alone explained nothing. Their silent sentinel could only prompt those who came by to revisit that day, to watch in their mind again as the Jordan parted, to be mesmerized again at what God was doing, to remember the glory, to re-experience the wonder, and to feel a fresh wave of faith that their God could do anything. The rocks couldn't remember, and none of them could tell the story of what happened that day. Without a "memory" to share, the rocks are no longer a "memorial." They're just a pile of rocks.

Rocks with Broken Hearts?

If, somehow, those rocks had been granted a heart and the ability to feel, their hearts would have been broken, because God's people eventually stopped coming, stopped bringing their kids, stopped telling the stories, and ceased to renew His power in their lives. Then they were no longer a memorial—just a lifeless bunch of stones.

Fast forward now to the holiday we call Memorial Day, a day when our monuments are highlighted and the sacrifices made by so many valiant men and women to protect our freedoms is recognized. If we strip that sacred day in our heritage from personal contact with its memories, then its monuments mean nothing. Our symbols have no voice of their own; and whether it's a cross hanging around our neck, or a statue in a park, or the picture of a loved one in a uniform, if we cut off the memories and stop telling the stories, then we cut off the meaning, and they're not really memorials anymore. If Memorial Day is just another day off and another excuse to grill hotdogs, then we've turned it into nothing more than another meaningless "pile of rocks."

A Long Road to Freedom

On July 4, 1776, a young, upstart collection of colonies issued a declaration to the world that henceforth they would be a free and independent nation, whose people would be able to exercise rights given to them by God, including the right of self-determination and that they would have the liberty to govern themselves. The King of England had a radically different view of that announcement from those who made it, and instead of seeing it as a lofty and noble ideal worthy of celebratory trappings such as banners and fireworks, he envisioned fireworks of a different kind. What was a glorious "Declaration of Independence" on one side of the ocean was an arrogant and rebellious declaration of war on the other.

More than One Perspective ~

Freedom is a compelling concept, but it isn't limited to only one perspective. One man's idea of liberty may represent provocation for conflict to another, and the emotions driving some toward one course of action may be just as powerful in moving others in an opposing direction. A quest for freedom can become the most noble of causes, but the intense emotions attached to it can lend themselves to manipulation and seduction. Addicts learn every day that the pursuit of something that feels like freedom can result in the ultimate loss of the liberties that were sought in the first place.

Jesus had some things to say about this idea, and John records one of the most familiar of His comments on the subject: *Then Jesus said to those Jews who believed Him, "If you abide in My word, you are My disciples indeed. And you shall know the truth, and the truth shall make you free"* (John 8:31-32).

His detractors didn't like that. They resented the inference that they weren't already free; and even though Israel was a conquered and occupied Roman province at the time, they declared that they had never been in bondage to anyone. Interesting. Freedom is a term that can be, to say the very least, a bit paradoxical, and one that is often defined by very different perspectives.

Freedom—A Costly Acquisition ~

At any given moment, a battle is going on somewhere. Nations, tribes, races, ethnic groups, religious sects, and other assorted bands of people are continuously embroiled in conflicts over some perceived threat to some aspect of their personal or collective liberty. They battle over religion, ideology, economic policies, and a myriad of other issues and special interests. One side or the other, and sometimes both, declare that their actions—some of which involve horrific, humiliating, and murderous treatment of other human beings—are justified because they're done in the name of freedom.

A religious civil war has been raging for years in Iraq and Syria, and our minds and hearts are stunned by the stories of fanatical hatred and random brutality. School children have been abducted in Nigeria and, very likely, have been offered for sale as slaves. Oppression and persecution of Christians and certain sects of other religions are rampant around the globe and growing in this country on an almost daily basis.

Freedom is a sought after commodity and a powerful motivator everywhere. Huge crowds have taken to the streets all over the world, rebelling against some kind of bondage and seeking some coveted aspect of freedom. Human carnage stains the face of this planet in every quadrant—a majority of it created by someone's desperate and frantic effort to escape some set of circumstances or rid themselves of some kind of oppressive authority. Sadly, in all too many cases, their fight for freedom only succeeds in exchanging one definition of misery for another.

God's Distinctive Approach ~

God offers a concept of freedom that is radically different from that embraced by the general culture. The core principle is unfolded in the story of a former slave that the apostle Paul befriended during one of his visits to Rome. The slave's name was Onesimus, and he apparently decided that his only path to freedom was to escape and take his chances as a runaway. No details are given about the escape or how he managed to get to Rome or how he came to meet Paul, but his story (Philemon 1:1-25) reveals a vital truth about freedom.

The relationship Onesimus developed with Paul was that of a friend, not a servant or a slave, and the service he rendered was based on love and respect, not obligation. What Onesimus would not have known in the beginning was that Paul had another friend who also had a relationship with this rebellious slave. The other friend's name was Philemon, and he happened to be the runaway's former master. Paul's love for both men, and his commitment to uphold God's righteousness, led him to urge Onesimus to do the right thing, and return to his master (Philemon 1:8-16).

Though Philemon was Paul's friend, he did not use that relationship as leverage to get Onesimus legally freed. Instead, he sought for him a different kind of freedom. Paul asked only that Philemon receive him back not just as a servant, but in a new relationship, that of a brother. Onesimus returned to his master with nothing in his hand but a letter, but that letter affirmed two relationships that had the power to change everything. Paul had introduced Onesimus to Jesus Christ, and both of Onesimus' new found friends offered him something that was both priceless and unattainable by his own efforts.

Relationships Can Appear to Alter Nothing but Change Everything ~

On the surface, returning home changed nothing about the situation Onesimus had risked his life to escape. He was still a slave, and Philemon was still his master. He was still required to serve his master as directed, whether he liked it or not. The only differences in his life were relational, not circumstantial, but the impact of those relationships was profound.

Paul said to Philemon, *If then you count me as a partner, receive him as you would me. But if he has wronged you or owes anything, put that on my account* (Philemon 1:17-18). Jesus had said basically the same thing to God the Father on our behalf when He offered Himself on Calvary's cross.

Onesimus craved freedom and thought that running away was the only way to find it. His road to freedom was long and perilous, and the vital question is whether or not he found it. If he did, when was it? Was freedom being a runaway slave in Rome with a death sentence on his head? Or was it when he surrendered his life to God and willingly went back home to serve his master as though he were serving the Lord?

It's fascinating how our concept of freedom and our view of being a "servant" changes when God's redemptive love is applied. Oppression can become opportunity and overseers can become "family." How different would our circumstances look if we saw freedom through the lens of relationships instead of circumstances? Maybe the freedom we really crave is not found in running *from* those things we cannot change, but in running *to* the One who can change how we see everything.

A Zombie Nod to Halloween

We Christian writers tend to ignore Halloween, but since another one is coming up, maybe we ought to break with tradition and give some thought to cockroaches, and in particular, the question that all of us wonder about from time to time—Do cockroaches experience anxiety? Having pondered it now for several seconds, my conclusion about the matter is that they probably do not. Now in the interest of transparency, I confess a total lack of empirical evidence to support my conclusion, but political figures, nationally known journalists, and academic elites get away with that kind of thing every day, so I'm invoking the same privilege.

What If Roaches Do Worry?

If I'm wrong, and cockroaches really do worry about stuff, and if they happen to live in the Mekong Delta region of Thailand, then they should be having outright panic attacks. Case in point: a heretofore undiscovered wasp has been identified in the area whose venom turns cockroaches into little cockroach zombies.

The wasp, dubbed the Ampulex Dementor by its discoverers, flies around until it spots a juicy, unsuspecting cockroach. Then it zooms down and injects its zombie-inducing drug directly into a bunch of brain neurons that the roach happens to have in its belly. My research didn't reveal why a cockroach would be running around with its brains in its belly, but I'm sure it has a good reason.

Zombie Terror from the Air ~

Once the wasp zaps its poison into the hapless bug's "brain," the roach is pretty much history, although the impact isn't instantly lethal. The roach remains officially "alive" after the attack, but it loses the ability to control its own movements. Once the venom is injected, the wasp assumes total control and can calmly drag its prey off to some secluded place and munch on it at its leisure until there's nothing left. Then it flies off in search of another defenseless meal.

We're way too familiar with zombie stories in this culture, but this one in the bug world is a bit different. In the usual scenario, it's the "living dead" that are wobbling around inciting terror, but if this little bug drama were turned into a zombie movie, the villain would be the dreaded zombie-makers. The half-dead victims would only evoke compassion—a fact, by the way, that would doom the production for human audiences, because, let's face it, who could dredge up pity for a cockroach?

As captivating as the whole zombie-making wasp drama might be, there's something here more fascinating and relevant than a brief excursion into "bug-world" theater. Apparently, the notion of dead people being somehow reanimated and transformed into bizarre creatures has had a macabre appeal to people in every generation. The extensive list of zombie movies goes all the way back to 1932, and the genre boasts hundreds of screenplays, books, short stories, stage productions, and video games. Perhaps even more surprising is the fact that God addressed a similar kind of condition 2,000 years ago.

A Biblical Background?

Consider this: God refers to unbelievers as being *dead in trespasses and sins* (Ephesians 2:1). And again, He says of certain widows devoting their lives to the pursuit of pleasure as being dead while they live (1 Timothy 5:6). Granted, the New Testament isn't supporting the modern idea of zombies, but we do find interesting similarities in that whole "dead-but-living" state wherein people are motivated and controlled by selfish, destructive internal appetites.

We aren't cockroaches, but we do have an enemy whose presence and influence permeates the culture surrounding us. He isn't a wasp, but he has a poisoned sting, and is called the *prince of the power of the air* (Eph 2:2). His desire is to do to us the same thing that Asian wasp does to its victims, to inject his "venom" into our brains and render us as helpless and doomed as those Thailand cockroaches. Satan's lethal potion is a mixture of our natural desire for pleasure, blended with deceptive philosophies, false premises, and seductive promises. The toxic effects of that poison can render us unable to resist the self-destructive attitudes and behaviors controlled by the lies planted in our brains. The venom doesn't kill instantly, but it prevents reactions designed for self-protection and preservation. With those defenses disabled, the enemy, like the wasp, is free to suck the life out of his victims until nothing remains but a dead, empty shell.

But of course, we're sophisticated human beings. We don't act like darkness-loving, disease-spreading, scavenging consumers of garbage who run around carrying our brains in our belly ... Oh, wait. In light of some of our tendencies, maybe I should rethink that.

Good News!

But there's good news, and we can take heart, because we have something the cockroach doesn't have. We have a Savior, and He has an antidote. Jesus subjected Himself to the full force of the enemy's venom, and the blood He shed for us on the cross has the power to neutralize our adversary's sting, render his poison ineffective, and set us free.

When the specter of Halloween approaches, it's refreshing to know that in a world full of enemies, venom, and zombie cockroaches, there's still overcoming power and eternal life in Jesus.

Another Look at Re-Gifting

There are two distinct but often interrelated phenomena that are endemic to this time of year—"Secret Santas" and the process of re-gifting.

The Christmas season unleashes a virtual army of agents into the streets and lanes of our nation. Though called by various names, most know them as the Secret Santas. Their covert mission is to scour every nook and cranny in the immediate environment, and then if necessary, to exhaust the resources of countless websites and stores in search of anything that might have a prayer of meeting the assigned gifting standard established by their various dispatchers. They assume clever, non-threatening disguises like relatives, workmates, friends, clients, members of the church "family," and hobby group partners.

Then, once they have acquired their objective, they slip undetected into family gatherings, office parties, church socials, civic clubs, and every other affinity group imaginable. They blend in with the crowd until just the right moment. Then, abandoning all restraint, the veil comes off and the Secret Santa strikes. He or she (they aren't gender specific) approaches the target and presents the spoils of their work in a brightly wrapped package that looks deceptively attractive.

Christmas does have its challenges. In almost any group gathering, a Secret Santa could just walk up to you, grinning like a mule eating briars, and shove a gift in your hand. You could be taken totally off guard and left standing there with everybody waiting to see how excited you're going to be when you open it. Meanwhile, you're hoping that the expression you're struggling to create gets interpreted as breathless anticipation instead of a sudden onset of abdominal cramps. Either way, you're already convinced that this is not going to make it into your list of "cherished Christmas moments."

At a time like that, you might find hope in the Hallmark Channel. They offer dramatic demonstrations about 947 times from October to January that Christmas miracles do happen, so maybe your Secret Santa surprise will be something you really want. But sadly, in spite of all that Hallmark hope, the Christmas optimism usually fades at about the same rate as the beautiful wrapping paper morphs into worthless trash. Then, important questions begin to fill your mind as you gaze on your newfound treasure, questions like:

1) What on earth is this thing?
2) What would I ever do with it?
3) If there's some actual store that sells whatever this is, is returning it a possibility?
4) If the answer to #3 is yes, what are the odds that they will find out whether I kept it or not?
5) Is God punishing me, and if I repent, will it go away?
6) Is there anyone else I can "bless" with this and not totally wreck my whole relationship with them?

Let's face it. Re-gifting happens, and we should address it, because the process can harbor the ugly specter of "guilt issues." For instance, if I re-gift this thing, does it mean that I'm some kind of vanity-ridden, Secret Santa diva, only willing to accept gifts of a certain quality or price? Does it mean that I'm a Christmas bigot, unintentionally making unfair judgments about others' taste in gifts? And while we're playing the guilt game, how about this one—What would Jesus think of me if I gave something away that someone else has given me?

Actually, that's a good question. And here's another one. What if it was never the giver's intent that a gift be kept anyway? What if re-gifting was what the giver wanted all along? What if giving you a gift was the giver's way of providing you with something to give someone else? What if instead of just giving someone a box of cookies, for instance, the gift was a bag of flour, some milk and sugar, a few other required ingredients, and a note reminding them of how many folks don't have a cookie, but would really love one? What if our most priceless gifts were meant to provide us with something to give that we could never obtain on our own?

The Giver of every good and perfect gift (James 1:17) said this, *As each one has received a gift, minister it to one another, as good stewards of the manifold grace of God* (1 Peter 4:10). Imagine that. Peter makes it clear that God never intended for us to hoard the things we've received from Him, but to re-package them in some new wrapping and pass them on to someone else. Wouldn't it be a paradigm changer if we saw our most cherished things not as too priceless to give away, but as far too valuable to keep for ourselves?

God knew, and Mary would eventually discover, that the miraculous little gift she cradled in her arms was far too precious for her and Joseph alone. God didn't just send a box of cookies or a loaf of holiday bread, He sent all it took to feed a starving world. The only hope for her—and the world He came to save—lay in the pain of giving Him away. May God help us to do some re-gifting this Christmas like He designed it to be.

Christmas: Same Old Thing

Someone I had just met a few minutes earlier stopped our conversation almost in mid-sentence with an unexpected and out of context question. "Well," he said as he paused and looked at me intently, "I was wondering, just how old *are* you, anyway?" I wanted to say, "Old enough to know not to ask questions like that of people I just met," but thought better of it. Side-stepping it with a dose of sarcastic humor was briefly appealing, but I figured Jesus might not like that, either. So, honesty and openness won out and I reluctantly told him my age.

He cocked his head to one side for a moment as though deep in thought and said, "Hmm ... I would have figured you for at least ten years older than that." Then he followed it up with, "But don't take it the wrong way." "How many ways are there?" I wondered. The sudden wave of snappy retort possibilities created a gridlock in my brain that left me with a blank look and no response at all—which probably made me look even older.

The occasion didn't put "old" things in a positive light for me, especially the one I see in the mirror, but another perspective eventually occurred to me. If someone offered me a box of gold coins, for instance, that had been buried in the ground for 2000 years, I'm pretty sure I'd take it. I don't think I'd tell him to come back and see me when he could come up with something newer, more up to date, and easier to handle. Neither would I be offended if someone offered me an original manuscript of one of

Shakespeare's plays because it was old and hard to read. "Old" isn't always a deficit. Sometimes it's priceless.

Everything about it was already "old" when Christmas and I first met. My grandmother, who introduced me to Christmas, was already old at the time—well, at least from the perspective of a little boy who was probably half the age of her newest apron. Our cherished little "sit-about" decorations, and our collection of delicate ornaments, like the hands that gently unwrapped them every December, had been around for generations.

But for Grandma and me, "old" wasn't a problem. We didn't think of our Christmas stuff as "old" in the sense that it was outdated and no longer significant, or that age had diminished their role in our family's celebrations. Those little ceramic figures, worn from years of handling, and the fragile glass ornaments, and those strands of lights may have been old, but they were faithful. Well, OK … I must admit that the lights were afflicted with an attention-seeking disorder that was chronic, but after a little loving manipulation, they always came around.

Every year in early December, our old Christmas "stuff" emerged from its sanctified resting place in the back of the hall closet, and it never failed to work its special magic and transform our house. It was just a box of old stuff, but it never failed to change our world from drab and ordinary into something that felt bright, and new, and full of hope. Like Grandma, and like the Christmas story itself, our holiday things were old, but that didn't matter when they found their familiar December duty stations in our house. Their impact wasn't measured in terms of clocks and calendars, and the only effect that time seemed to have on them was to make them more special with every passing year.

As each Christmas season approaches, preachers, teachers, speakers, and writers all over the world will struggle to find some new slant on a story that's been around for over two millennia. Every syllable of the text will be scrutinized afresh, eyes will peer at the same changeless and familiar words, anxiously searching for something not really hidden, but somehow yet unseen. Prayers will implore divine help in finding some new insight, some fresh, stimulating new approach. Brains will be wracked for some previously unuttered thought that will help the story not seem so "old"—as though familiarity has rendered the astounding reality of the event itself somehow insufficient. Its profundity and simplicity can confound us. Children recite it, but this uncomplicated story is the inspired account of how the omnipotent God of all creation made His entrance into the world of human beings as one of us. It's overwhelming.

No wonder we obsess over every minor nuance, magnify immaterial details, and proceed to preach lengthy sermons about unverifiable subplots. How can we effectively elaborate on the event itself, when the meaning is far more extensive than we have the capacity to grasp? It's frustrating. This familiar and uncluttered story challenges us. Our best words barely escape the level of insult when compared to the simple ones He provided, yet we cannot stand in its presence and not feel compelled to speak, to write, to sing, to do something. Every year the truth calls us back to the core. So, we turn to the Gospels and wrestle to lay hold of the power of this "old" story every year, and every year we lose, and in the losing, we win. We cannot do it justice, and we cannot let it be. Though it won't let us walk away feeling quite as proud as we otherwise might, or standing quite as tall as we'd like, we never seem to leave it having our weakness feel so strong.

Unwrapping a Christmas Mystery

My grandmother was one of sweetest, most considerate people I ever knew—normally. But something happened to all that whenever someone handed her a Christmas present with her name on it, and memories of those times trigger flashbacks not unlike an episode of PTSD—at least as seen through the eyes of a preadolescent kid. Being a kid in our house back then meant being subjected to the painful, adult interpretations of what it meant for kids to be "patient." The standard Christmas application of the torturous term in our family included forcing us kids to wait until the "older adults" had opened their presents before being allowed to even get near our own.

A Hall of Fame Poker Face ~

My grandmother was the reigning queen of the older adult category in our house. Watching her handle presents would have been more bearable if she acted like she had any interest at all in ever getting to whatever was inside. Nothing about her ever revealed the slightest clue that she thought the package had anything of value in it. Grandma never played cards, but poker players nationwide would have drooled at the chance of having a poker face like hers. You'd have a better chance of finding hints of positive optimism on the face of a bomb disposal guy in a race with a ticking timer, than Grandma with a Christmas present in her clutches.

Didn't she realize that it had been a whole year since the last time she'd had her hands on one? Instead of exhibiting something normal, like maybe some happy anticipation, all she ever wanted to do was relate shock and astonishment that the giver had actually relinquished money to buy something for her. Then she'd reiterate how incomprehensible and unnecessary such a sacrifice was, casting unavoidable aspersion on the financial judgment of whoever gave it. Some of us in the room heartily agreed and wished they hadn't given her anything at all.

Ahead of Her Time ~

Grandma was at least four generations ahead of the compulsive recyclers that fill our land today. She would begin the unwrapping process by untying every ribbon as though it actually felt pain. I wished there had been some worry about my pain level. It was never enough in my young mind to just pull a ribbon off. Oh no, ribbons and bows had to be removed with such care that if they were ever actually used again, the next recipient wouldn't have the slightest suspicion that they had been rescued and restored.

Then there was the paper. Plastic surgeons lifting the facial epidermis of a sixty-year-old patient with significant legal resources had nothing on the care Grandma displayed. Watching it was exasperating. I wanted to collapse onto the floor into a full-blown meltdown fit, except that fits weren't allowed for kids, especially at Christmas. Fits were reserved for adults facing real crises, like not being able to find their car keys.

Moving forward, many relate our Christmas gift-giving these days with the offerings of the wise men, but while that may feel spiritually invigorating, most of what we practice these days is more the product of fertile imaginations and slick advertising than anything directly derived from the Scriptural record. Widespread celebrations of Christmas didn't begin to be popularized in the western world until the start of the Victorian Age, beginning in the early 1800s. Until then, Christians may have observed it, but it was not a widely recognized or celebrated holiday.

Even though Christmas had become the most widely celebrated holiday of the year by the end of that century, wrapping gifts as we do now was still not a widespread practice. In those early days, Christmas gifts were most likely to be placed in the recipient's shoes or stockings. Concealing gifts wasn't a new idea, but the popular use of wrapping paper didn't begin until a couple of brothers named Hall stumbled on the idea, almost by accident, in 1917, and it caught on. Ever hear of Hallmark?

Wrapping—Enhancing the Joy of Discovery ~

Wrapping gifts in ways that conceal what they are can be a lot of fun. It helps to elevate the sense of excitement and anticipation and prolongs the joy of the moment for both the giver and receiver. There's something inherently uplifting and optimistic about unwrapping a gift or watching someone we love discover what we've given (except possibly for folks like Grandma). The more valuable the gift, the greater the joy for both. God knew that long before we ever figured it out.

We find the idea of concealment and discovery interwoven in the New Testament use of the term *mystery*. The term as used in the Bible doesn't carry the meaning we often apply today, that of something that can't be figured out or understood. God used it to indicate that the full identity, the real meaning, and the ultimate value of something were *yet to be discovered*. That idea is nowhere more profoundly presented than in Jesus Christ Himself. Paul repeatedly used the term *mystery* in reference to Jesus. To the Colossian believers, he referred to Jesus' coming as *the mystery which has been hidden from ages and from generations, but now has been revealed to His saints* (Colossians 1:26).

> A mystery is something yet to be discovered.
> ~

A Glorious Place to Start ~

I find it fascinating that the angel said to the shepherds that they would find the Baby *wrapped in swaddling cloths* (Luke 2:12). God gave us a gift in Jesus, and the value of that gift was not evident from the outside. The real gift was wrapped in more than simple swaddling cloths. It was the glory of God Himself wrapped in human form. Like the shepherds, we're invited to find Him and to begin the process of discovering who He really is and what He means to each of us. An eternity of Christmas mornings will not suffice to unwrap it all, but it can be a *glorious* place to start.

Part III
Right Side Up Responses to Cultural Conflicts and Political Issues

Introduction: Reactions to the Challenge of an Oppositional World

Whether I liked it or not, Dusty was my wake-up call. He came with an alarm feature that alerted him when humans were enjoying a moment of pleasant, peaceful inactivity, and it apparently irritated him. He could sense it from any other room in the house, and within seconds, he'd pounce his fat self on the bed and be on top of me, prodding at me with his paws and purring like a feline Harley Davidson.

Dusty could have made me aware of his presence in ways that would not have gotten him the response he was after. Instead, he developed what I'd call his "purr and stir" method, which made dozing off again impossible, thus rendering any benefit from my snooze alarm null and void. He devised a way to make himself impossible to ignore and kept at it until he got what he wanted. It was a lesson in persistence worth remembering.

In today's culture, we may have become so accustomed to encountering "upside down thinking" that it doesn't rouse us anymore. We're used to conflict. We're used to tabloid headlines, TV shows, and movies promoting anti-Christian sentiments. We're used to groups of people questioning religious liberties. The danger is that we can become so accustomed to ways of thinking that are contrary to God's system of love, justice, and holiness that we "fall asleep." We may miss a chance to promote God's "right side up thinking."

If we've been lulled into a sleep of inactivity, what can we do? Wake up and suit up.

> *It is high time to awake out of sleep ...*
> *The night is far spent, the day is at hand.*
> *Therefore let us cast off the works of darkness,*
> *and let us put on the armor of light.*
> Romans 13:11-12

Our spiritual enemy has not found new sins with which to tempt us, just new methods. His mission is to wreak as much destruction as he can in the time he has left.

Since the time of early church, God's reaction to the enemy's efforts to lull us into his dark world has been to send out an army of light. In every generation, He has dispatched His faithful servants to declare and display His love and truth; to pray and fight for the redemption of every man, woman, and child; and to continue His work through the power of His Spirit. All of us who have received Jesus Christ are a part of that "army of Light." We have been graciously called to Him and delivered from our misery and darkness. Not only that, we have already been conveyed into the *kingdom of the Son of His love* (Colossians 1:13). Our enemy continues to work around us every day, and because other souls hang in the balance, it's not a time to sleep.

My prayer is that the material in this section might prod all of us not only to be involved in our culture, but to do some "stirring and purring" of our own. If we can adopt some of Dusty's persistence, maybe we can help to awaken others, arouse some new recruits, and encourage them to *cast off the works of darkness* (Romans 13:12) and join us.

Wanna Hear Me Play My Smoke Detector?

The stillness of a typically peaceful night at the Gallagher compound was destroyed recently when the wee morning stillness was shattered by a sudden, piercing, and thoroughly annoying sound. It was a sound that produces a reaction in one's head that is akin to whatever it is that goes off inside a cat when you see it suddenly explode into a three-foot vertical leap and proceed to perform midair maneuvers that would make Olympic divers and gymnasts hang their heads in shame. And just in case you're wondering, I did not attempt to replicate that kind of performance that night, but not because the urge wasn't there. It was only because the movements that the adrenalin surge were calling for in my head would have been physiologically impossible for normal humans.

The Culprit ~

The auditory terrorist invading my sleep and seriously threatening my sanity was a smoke detector. The ear-piercing noise it produced seemed to be coming from everywhere. Our house is constructed so that four of those little electronic banshees were positioned close enough to one another so that in the midst of the screeching, echoing, auditory nightmare they create, it's virtually impossible to determine which one is the culprit without multiple trips up and down a ladder. It was not the first event giving rise to my suspicions that perhaps our house was designed by architects operating under demonic influence. I'm convinced that if we allowed the military to incorporate these devices as part of our "enhanced interrogation" protocols, we'd have terrorists fighting with each other over who got to be next in line to spill their guts about everything they knew.

In spite of the personal drama that my device caused for no apparent reason, the presence of smoke detectors is a good thing. As beneficial as they are, their invention was really quite unintentional. A would-be inventor named Walter Jaeger set out in the late 1930s to create a detector for poison gas. To his initial disappointment, he discovered that the principle upon which he was basing his invention was flawed. He had hypothesized that his sensor mechanism would detect the ionized air in the toxic gas and trigger enough of a fluctuation in the electric current to activate the warning signal. It seemed like a good idea theoretically; it's just that it didn't work. The poison gas had no effect at all on his sensor.

Accidental Origins ~

Confronted with the realization that his work had failed, he sat back and lit a cigarette to reflect on the situation. When the smoke from his cigarette contacted the sensor, he noticed that there was a change in the electrical current, and the modern smoke detector was born. Now, ninety-three percent of the homes in America have a smoke detector of some kind installed, and multitudes of lives have been saved since they were introduced.

I recall a news story from earlier this year that was beyond tragic. A parent and three children were killed when their home caught fire in the night. That would be heartbreaking on any basis, but it was even more troubling with the revelation that there were alarms installed in the house, but they apparently didn't work. Had the smoke detectors worked, that family would almost certainly be alive today.

The use and value of smoke detectors is predicated on the realization that the danger of fire is real, prevalent, and almost always unanticipated. They are simple devices and as modern tech devices go, they aren't very "smart." You can't call anybody on it, and the "tweets" it sends won't get you any new followers. It won't connect you with Facebook or text your friends or do a selfie to show off your new hairdo. It has only one purpose. It's all about fire. They're not put in place to google the history of heat and conduct a digital discussion about the origins and sociological implications of fire. They have one job, and it's not to provide entertainment. If the volume and tone of their alarm isn't, well ... "alarming," they are totally worthless. And by the way, they aren't designed to hang around and wait until they feel the heat to respond either. They start screeching at the slightest evidence of smoke.

Another Kind of Fire Alarm Meant for a Slumbering Nation ~

Consider this. God's prophets have often been called upon to perform a function for their people not unlike that of a spiritual smoke detector. They were sent to sound an alarm, not to radiate soothing messages to enhance the nation's slumber. They were put in place because there was a threat, and that threat was real. God's judgment was imminent, and implications were disastrous. Like good smoke detectors, God's prophets didn't wait to feel the heat. They were activated because the "smoke"—those symptoms that judgment had already begun—were already detectable, and immediate action was necessary if people were to be saved. Sadly, the smoke detector's capacities are limited. It can't drag a family out of bed and haul them to safety, and God's messengers face the same limitations.

It's hard to be one of God's smoke detectors—we'd rather be God's smart phone. Smoke detectors just make raucous, irritating noises, and we prefer more soothing sounds. You've probably already noticed that smoke detectors aren't popular centerpieces for parties and gatherings. Think of it this way, how many times have you been invited over to a friend's house to sit around and listen to his smoke detector? And how many times have you bought a ticket to attend a concert just to hear a guy play his fire alarm for two hours? In spite of the fact that they don't produce the kind of sound we want to hear, when one goes off and we realize that the fire is real, we're suddenly deeply grateful that we heard it, and thank God that the raucous, irritating sound we didn't like has just become our salvation.

God's Purpose Is Clear ~

God's purpose in sending His "smoke detectors" is not to punish people, or because He delights in irritating them. He sends them because He loves those who are ignorant of the danger and are dreaming their way to disaster. God wants them to escape while there is still time, and warnings delivered in soft, relaxing sounds won't accomplish that. All of us love sounds that make us feel good whether they're coming from electronic devices or people, and we happily gather around to hear them. But when danger is imminent and threatened destruction is real, something more unsettling is called for, something more like the prophet Micah, who was sent to be one of God's smoke detectors. He said:

> *Therefore I will wail and howl ... I will make a wailing like the jackals and a mourning like the ostriches ... for it* [God's judgment] *has come to Judah; it has come to the gate of My people—to Jerusalem.* (Micah 1:8-9)

Micah wasn't sent to please an audience and garner applause, and he wasn't interested in approval ratings—just in saving his nation from certain judgment.

Here's a suggestion. In light of the dangerous level of immorality and anti-Christian sentiment permeating our nation, instead of hanging out and watching the game this weekend, what if we had a few friends over and checked to see if our smoke detectors are still working?

BOLO for Goldilocks

Memories of fairy tales and other such stories from my childhood are pretty vague except for two. "Hansel and Gretel" remains in the traumatically unforgettable category in light of its dual impact on my life. This singular literary experience introduced me to the possibility that cannibalistic witches with a taste for young kids like me could be lurking in the woods behind our house—and to what it was like to have recurrent nightmares.

Here though, I want to focus on the story of "Goldilocks and the Three Bears." It seemed at the time to be a rather pointless tale with no obvious enduring quality, but it stuck in my head anyway and at least reinforced my profound conviction that normal human beings, especially kids, should not be allowed to go wandering in the woods.

Strange Family—Strange Tale ~

As you might recall, the Goldilocks story centers on a family of bears with strange names—"Mama Bear," "Papa Bear," and "Baby Bear." Cute, but not very imaginative. One might be left to wonder what happened when "Baby Bear" turned 40 and weighed 437 pounds. Would he or she still be called "Baby," or would the name evolve through ensuing stages of development and become "Toddler Bear," "Pre-Adolescent Bear," "Teen Bear," and so forth? And what were "Mama" and "Papa" Bear called prior to having offspring? Fairy tales can be frustrating like that.

In any case, we assume these anthropomorphic bears lived in a middle-class woodland neighborhood where they enjoyed a lifestyle that most of their species don't get. They had convenient appliances, like stoves, and they seemed to enjoy cooking, sitting around in chairs, and sleeping in beds.

The story opens with the Bear family about to sit down to a lovely meal of porridge when they discovered that the stuff was way too hot to eat. The prospect of risking blistered lips or sitting around for half an hour blowing on their porridge bowls (a frustrating endeavor for bears, since the whole pucker thing is so hard for them) led someone to suggest an alternative. It was agreed that taking a power walk through the woods while their porridge cooled would be far better than slobbering all over their lunch trying to blow on it. All in all, it was a very *family* kind of scene, very heartwarming—and downright "*Abearicana.*"

Mysterious Blonde Invader ~

Enter Goldilocks. Literally. We don't know much about her beyond the inference that she's not quite an adult yet, and given that her name wasn't "Brownilocks," we figure she's probably blonde. There's no evidence that she had to pick a lock, kick the door in, or crawl through an unsecured window, which suggests that bears living in middle-class woodland neighborhoods aren't concerned about home invasions and don't lock their doors.

It's clear from the start that Goldilocks is a girl who doesn't balk at violating boundaries, and once inside, is unperturbed about getting into other people's personal stuff, even their food. With no concern for propriety, Goldilocks proceeds to plunder through the Bear family's resources and lay claim to anything that might satisfy her appetite or contribute to her personal comfort. And we might add to her profile that she is critical, opinionated, demanding, and hyperattentive to her own sensitivities.

Busted ~

Eventually, the bears return, and Goldilocks is busted. They discover that the narcissistic little interloper has invaded their home, eaten some of their food, flopped around on all their furniture, and with an in-your-face kind of arrogance, is sound asleep in one of their beds. I don't really recall what happened next, but given the twisted imagination evident in children's horror classics like "Hansel and Gretel," maybe the bears decided to throw out the porridge and eat her instead. Of course, that would have wrecked the whole heartwarming, family-friendly thing, but would have added another solid argument for keeping kids out of the woods.

We'll go for the moral high ground here and assume the bears didn't lean toward *Goldiburgers* for dinner that night, and that the girl was resourceful enough to escape. What happened after that is anybody's guess. Maybe the police got her DNA off the porridge bowl and connected her to a whole string of woodland home invasions. Maybe she was caught, tried as an adult, and ended up sporting an orange jumpsuit and spending her days filing lawsuits claiming that prison food was "too cold," that prison chairs were "too hard," that prison cells were "too small," that prison pillows were "too soft," and that absolutely nothing was "just right."

Back in Circulation ~

But truth be told, speculating on her past history is not the issue here. We need to consider sending out one of those notices the police call a BOLO—Be-On-the-Look-Out—because Goldilocks is back in circulation. If she did get incarcerated after invading the Bear residence, jail time didn't help. She's just as invasive and self-centered as ever and still loves to go after unsecured things in vulnerable territories, and we're seeing her influence spread dramatically, especially in our churches.

> BOLO
> Be-On-the-
> Look-Out
> ~

Invading territory that belongs to someone else and claiming squatter's rights to whatever she can find is the modern-day Goldilocks' classic modus operandi. That she has no valid claim to whatever she goes after doesn't bother her at all, and her guiding principles go no deeper than her personal preferences and physical comfort.

A New Territory ~

Churches fascinate Goldilocks. She loves the fact that the doors are always open, and there's lots of stuff to try out, especially around "the holidays." If things aren't "just right," her inclination is to either trash them or exert her influence to get them adjusted, like she invariably does with the Christmas story, for instance.

The true story of Christmas grates against Goldilocks' sensibilities, given her insistence on rejecting the uncomfortable, spurning the undesirable, and avoiding the unsuitable. For her, everything about Mary and Joseph's journey is just "too" something—too treacherous, too far, too hard, too costly, too dark, too unfair, and too painful. Since she finds none of it feeling "just right," she sidesteps all that unacceptable inconvenience in favor of a Christmas that's all about fun things, bright things, colorful things, and things you get without having to pay for them.

The Underlying Problem ~

Goldilocks can't help doing that. It's who she is, and therein lies both the core of the problem and the potential solution. An often overlooked but unavoidable realization in the original story is that Goldilocks was not, and never had been, a bear—and thus, was not a part of the family whose home she invaded.

That's relevant because whether it's a Christmas issue or other elements in the realm of Christianity, there are things that belong uniquely to the "family." When those who are not a part of the family, and who are only seeking their own comfort and satisfaction, intrude and begin to exercise family privileges, it results in conflict and confusion.

God's Solution ~

God unveiled His ingenious plan for resolving the problem to an interloping Pharisee in the third chapter of John. Jesus basically told him he would never be allowed to come into the Father's home and partake of His stuff unless he was part of the family. Being born again (John 3:3-6) was God's way to accomplish that. Jesus' sacrifice made it possible for God to take outsiders lost in a vain quest for self-satisfaction and make them part of the family. His death and resurrection provide a basis for transforming all of us selfish, grasping interlopers and turning us into sons and daughters who each has his or her own place at the table with His forever family. When God takes "Goldilocks clones" like us and makes us part of His family, it's incredible how many things suddenly become "just right."

It's Not a Battle Cruiser Anymore

Stories heralding love's invincibility fill libraries and databases all over the world. Compared to some of the monstrous foes that love is said to have brought down on behalf of those it favored, David's little romp with Goliath can seem almost insignificant.

Love's exploits are a wellspring of material for every form of artistic expression known to man. And if human accolades weren't enough, God Himself declared with divine authority that *love never fails* (1 Corinthians 13:8). It sounds like maybe the Beatles might have been right when they suggested that we could have a "slam-dunk" victory over anything the world could throw at us— "All we need is love, love, love."

Reality Contradicts Love's Claims ~

The problem is that the world around us doesn't reflect that. It reveals a largely narcissistic, consumer-oriented culture obsessed with the pursuit of personal pleasure, mesmerized by self-awareness, and convinced that anarchy is the pathway to freedom. We find a people plagued with violence and subjected continuously to accounts of conflict, fear, hatred, greed, lust, anxiety, selfish ambition, and prejudice. Altogether, the social and relational indicators are more suggestive of a state of love deprivation than one of blessing and positive contribution. Granted, a few accounts of love's triumph over life's challenges emerge from time to time, but they pale in comparison to the mounting chronicles of pain and loss piling up everywhere we look.

This sobering contrast to love's claims that reality unveils, calls into question all those reports of its stellar reputation. It prods us to ask whether we've been duped. Has love's fabled overcoming power been misrepresented? Have we somehow stripped it of its power? Have we buried Superman under a wagonload of Kryptonite and then blamed him for not saving us?

Taking the Search to the Source ~

Our questions ultimately lead us back to love's originator. To separate love from God, or God from love is to dishonestly represent either one. Love isn't something God does. It is who He is (1 John 4:8). Any apparent failure of love to demonstrate the overcoming power attributed to it, is not due to any defect in its design. The problem is that we have done to love what my grandson did to one of his favorite LEGO® creations, a huge *Star Wars* battle cruiser.

He was hyperventilating with excitement when he got it, and he invested hours of work to assemble its hundreds of tiny, carefully engineered pieces. The completed project worked perfectly, and he showed it off with joyful exuberance, demonstrating that every one of its numerous functions worked exactly as originally designed.

It's Costly to Dissect God's Design for Love ~

During another visit months later, I asked about his battle cruiser. He took me to his room and showed me a large box full of LEGO® pieces and a few small, nondescript, vehicle-like creations that he had invented. "Where's the starship?" I asked. "Well," he said, "this is it. I just took it apart and used the pieces to make some other stuff."

The cruiser's parts were all there, but nobody would ever mistake that disconnected LEGO® dumping ground for the complex starship it had been earlier, and there was no way those disconnected pieces could perform any of the functions that were part of its original plan. Dissecting God's design for love to scavenge its more appealing pieces for use as a personal toy, carries the same cost and has the same result.

In one of the most eloquent declarations of the power of love ever penned, Paul concluded with this. *For I am persuaded that neither death nor life, nor angels nor principalities nor powers, nor things present nor things to come, nor height, nor depth, nor any other created thing, shall be able to separate us from the love of God which is in Christ Jesus our Lord* (Romans 8:38-39). The last seven words of that declaration hold the key to most of our questions about why love doesn't seem to be working so well in our society, and maybe in our own lives as well.

Don't Wreck the Original ~

In dismantling his battle cruiser to use its pieces to make some other kind of vehicle, my grandson wrecked the original. The love God designed suffers the same fate when we pull it apart to create our own version. All of the intricate nuances and mystical complexities that work in harmony to make love the profound, overcoming force that God has shown it to be, were perfected and complete "in Christ." All of the elements granting love its invincibility reside "in Christ." To dismantle those elements and remove them from Him leaves only a disconnected box of impotent emotional pieces.

Claiming love's attractive qualities and rejecting those that often hurt is a human tendency that wrecks love's original design, and leaves it functionally disabled. Love with the power to subdue every foe and to rise in triumph after every battle, also has parts that demand sacrifice, sorrow, and tears. Love is a multifaceted, composite creation, not a menu of random parts, and as Paul affirmed, it resides wholly "in" Christ and is only available in Him.

> Love resides wholly "in" Christ and is only available in Him.
> ~

If we cut love up and strip it away from the One in whom it dwells, it won't matter what we call the pieces. None of its weapons will work, and it won't be a "battle cruiser" anymore.

This is My commandment,
that you love one another
as I have loved you.
John 15:12

Time to Clear the Air?

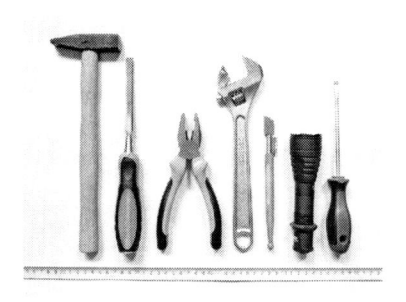

Have you noticed that those big home improvement warehouse stores are more than incredible repositories of stuff that guys feel compelled to buy but don't really need, will never use, and eventually let go in a yard sale for a tenth of the original cost? And that they also harbor a veritable Wikipedia of information and advice, thanks to an apparent abundance of outside volunteers whose contributions, we might add, are neither authorized nor controlled by the store's management?

Introducing the NHSHPSW~

I refer to those folks as "Non-Certified Home Store Handy Person Social Workers" (NHSHPSWs). These people patrol the aisles in no identifiable pattern and are intent on helping you whether you like it or not. They frequent the store when they're not making their own YouTube video about using duct tape to repair just about anything.

Their intervention often begins with an impromptu monologue about some project disaster they just experienced, replete with "colorful" descriptive terms you never wanted to hear and intimate details about the impact on their marital relations, their financial portfolio, and their gastro-intestinal wellbeing. About the time you're becoming convinced that for these guys, "DIY" doesn't mean "Do-It-Yourself," it means "Destroyed-It-Yesterday," they abandon the tale of their own train wreck in order to explain, at no extra charge, that the thing you're looking at and have come there to purchase will never work.

An Intervention in Action ~

An NHSHPSW ambushed me among the HVAC air filters recently, because I was guilty of two critical infractions of protective protocol. First, I stopped walking and stood still for over eighteen seconds—that draws them like a laser beam on a smart bomb target. Then I made matters worse by carelessly allowing an expression to creep onto my face that normal people would interpret as just a guy trying to decide what to buy. The NHSHPSW zeros in on that same expression and thinks, "That guy doesn't look like he knows what he's doing, and he's liable to end up hurting himself if I don't intervene." So, without wasting time on trivial opening lines like, "Hi there ...", the NHSHPSW sprang into action. The conversation that followed went something like this ...

NHSHPSW (pointing to the air filter in front of me): "You're not gonna get *that* one are you?"

Me: "Well, I'm just checking them out and haven't decided which one I'm going with yet."

NHSHPSW: "Well, you're gonna need to keep away from that junk and get that hypoallergenic one over there."

Me: "Really? I usually just buy whichever one is cheaper."

NHSHPSW: "No, no, no ... you can't be thinking like that. There's junk floatin' around in the air these days that'll flat-out kill you."

Me: "That's disturbing."

NHSHPSW: "Yeah, but you see that one over there? That one's got that micro-whatchacallit stuff in it, and that'll suck up junk you can't even see."

Me: "Hmmm ... I don't know—what if I just buy the cheap one and encourage the family to cut back on breathing?"

NHSHPSW: Blank stare.

My would-be rescuer's effort to save me from death by cheap air filter did include a valid point, and it prompted me to think about air filters in a way that I might not have otherwise. He was right when he said that there are dangerous things in the air all around us, but there are greater threats to be concerned about than dust particles and pet dander. Other invisible things use the air we breathe for transportation, too—like sound waves.

Filters Desperately Needed ~

For example, I observed an exchange between two people at a fast food restaurant recently. I'd call it a conversation, but that would be far too generous. For a few minutes, they turned the atmosphere into a verbal sewer, filling the air with a disgusting display of foul language and profanity. Their words were uttered in harsh, angry tones and were accompanied by sarcastic, snarky attitudes on both sides.

Sadly, hearing filthy words in public places these days is an all-too-common experience. It has become endemic to living in America, and we hear it virtually everywhere. It makes the whole idea of air filters take on a broader connotation than the one I had in mind at the hardware store and reminds me that God had some things to say about filtering our words. Consider these:

> *Let your speech always be with grace, seasoned with salt, that you may know how you ought to answer each one.* (Colossians 4:6)

> *Let no corrupt word proceed out of your mouth, but what is good for necessary edification, that it may impart grace to the hearers.* (Ephesians 4:29)

And to His opponents, Jesus said this:

> *Brood of vipers! How can you, being evil, speak good things? For out of the abundance of the heart the mouth speaks. A good man out of the good treasure of his heart brings forth good things, and an evil man out of the evil treasure brings forth evil things. But I say to you that for every idle word men may speak, they will give account of it in the day of judgment. For by your words you will be justified, and by your words you will be condemned.* (Matthew 12:34-37)

Scriptures like that, and many others, used to be proclaimed without hesitation or apology from the pulpits across this land. They worked with our conscience to create spiritual "filters," and they helped to keep the atmosphere in our nation cleaner. When God's directives were proclaimed and taken seriously, the impact and benefits were widespread and powerful. Unlike the confining and controlling strategy of today's "Political Correctness Police," God's design was not simply to place a muzzle on our lips and dictate what we could and could not say. As Jesus clearly taught, the problem with our mouth begins with the heart. God's "filtering system" involves a spiritual transformation at the point where the contaminating thoughts and words originate.

Toxic Impact of Missing Filters ~

Have you noticed that our national filter is getting more and more clogged? If we remove God from the public arena, we will remove our only effective personal and social filtering system. As the spiritual filters have diminished or disappeared, the standards of verbal decorum have declined along with them, and the linguistic atmosphere has become more and more filled with moral impurities. Symptoms of their toxic influence quickly became epidemic, moving naturally from words to behavior. Verbal disrespect becomes physical abuse; sexually explicit words become sexual coercion and assault; violent speech leads to random physical attacks.

Traditional family values once played a protective role, and they were especially helpful through those years when children develop a moral and ethical consciousness. Those values have faced systematic challenges in the past few decades and in many cases have been restricted in favor of public policies promoting inclusiveness and diversity. When these filters are damaged or missing altogether, the particles that are allowed in may seem small and harmless initially, but their cumulative impact in the long term can be devastating.

My hardware store advisor wisely suggested that I not cut corners on filtering the air in my house. In America, it appears to me that we are in danger of doing far worse. On one hand, the widespread application of effective spiritual "filters," like family prayer, regular church attendance, and recognizing an authoritative source for moral judgment, is on the decline. But more sobering and dangerous than that is the tendency to declare that those "filters" are the problem, not the trash they were designed to protect us from.

So ... I'm not an official NHSHPSW, but maybe it's time to ask, "How's the filtering system in your house?"

Is Freedom Just Another Word?

In 1971, Kris Kristofferson recorded a slightly altered Janis Joplin song that had a particularly haunting line about freedom. He described freedom as the result of having nothing left in your life that you could lose, and concluded that while freedom was basically worthless, at least it was free. In spite of its melancholy treatment in that song, freedom is and always will be a subject with powerful implications.

Good News for Some Can Be Bad News for Others ~

Every July Fourth, we celebrate America's declaration to the world that from that date in 1776, America would be free and independent of British authority. The hunger for freedom was strong in this fledgling nation, and its people were determined to assert their God-given rights, including the right of self-determination. You may recall that the King of England at that time was not so impressed with their announcement. Somehow he missed the whole thing about it being a declaration worth celebrating. To put it in family terms, it was like kids saying to an abusive parent who was exploiting them for his own profit, "That's it ... We're moving out."

He interpreted it as a declaration worthy of lethal repercussions and was willing to commit his nation's military might in the effort to stomp out what was, to him, an intolerable affront to his throne and his nation's leadership in the world. Imagine that. One man's liberation is another man's provocation. Either way, freedom is a powerful idea. It can represent the most noble of causes, but it can also be misconstrued and misunderstood. Freedom is an idea that can lend itself to manipulation and seduction, and one that can be twisted so as to result in the ultimate loss of the very liberties that were sought in the first place.

Wherever you find it, freedom's DNA is always laced with inflammatory possibilities because it has no definition except in reference to some form of real or perceived bondage. The elements of conflict, then, are already in place when the idea of freedom begins to emerge, and the intensity of the desire for it correlates directly with the degree to which that bondage has begun to feel like bondage.

Freedom Isn't Tangible until It Touches Us ~

Janis Joplin's lyric feels disturbing to many of us "freedom-loving Americans," but is there some modicum of truth buried in it? It could be argued that freedom really is, after all, just a metaphysical concept, a word with no concrete "thing" that it defines, like a machine, or a weapon, or even a piece of technology. Freedom represents no tangible resource, no arsenal that it controls, no army that it commands, and no central organization from which it projects power or delegates authority. Freedom is just a construct—just an idea—and if it remains only that, it accomplishes nothing. As an isolated term, it doesn't rise up to challenge anything or change anything. That kind of freedom doesn't threaten tyrants or antagonize oppressors.

When freedom is left disembodied, the conclusion Kris and Janis presented is accurate. To the degree that it's nothing more than a piece of political vernacular, there is no great price attached to claiming it and no significant accomplishment associated with laying hold of it. Freedom's value will always be determined by the cost required to obtain it and the courage demanded to protect and preserve it.

But when the idea invades the mind and heart of a human being in bondage, something remarkable happens. Freedom becomes something else, something living, something powerful, something invincible, and something that threatens oppression like nothing else can. Once firmly entrenched in a human heart, freedom will rise up in defiance of odds that are overwhelming. When the word becomes embodied in men and women, it ceases to be just a word.

Freedom in that state transcends mere vocabulary and transforms those it indwells. When freedom breathes in human lungs and beats in human hearts, the weak find new strength, despair gives way to hope, courage displaces fear, trembling cowards become valiant warriors, and no longer can it be said that freedom is worthless—but at that point, it is also no longer "free." When freedom comes to life in men, the idea is incendiary, claiming it is reactionary, and asserting it is revolutionary.

> Freedom breathes in human lungs and beats in human hearts.

Love of Freedom Can Reverse the Target of Terror ~

Jesus Christ embodied a kind of freedom that stands in defiant opposition to the bondage of the world, and He offered it to all who would follow Him. *If the Son makes you free,* He said, *you shall be free indeed* (John 8:36). Our world is infected with oppressors who seek to enslave others and to paralyze us with fear. Some with their bombs and bullets, and others with threats of political, social, or religious repercussions for resisting their godless and intrusive regulations.

What if on July Fourth, we opened our hearts afresh to the God who alone promises freedom? Perhaps we'd see reignited that powerful embodiment of liberty that built this nation and defended it for over 200 years.

When those who are abused come to cherish freedom like Patrick Henry did in 1776, it is the oppressors and tyrants who tremble. When "Give me liberty or give me death" lives in the hearts of God's people, it is the terrorists who are terrorized. May God help us to fan that flame again and purge this nation of the crippling bondage of cowardice and fear.

Crocheted Words and Verbal Doilies

I wasn't sure what to expect as she pulled the string over my thumb, wrapped it around my forefinger, and put the little hook thingy in my hand. Grandma was about to teach her five-year-old grandson how to crochet. It didn't seem like a big deal at the time, and at least it gave me something to do. I was intrigued by the idea of learning this curious-looking process, and since Grandma was pretty good at it, I figured I'd be cranking out all kinds of fancy-looking stuff by dinner time—not my only misconception about the art of crocheting.

Grandma stuck with it until I learned, an effort for which I have since forgiven her. After all, she only had boys to work with, and she had probably already taught us all the "guy" stuff she knew by that time. It didn't hit me till later that I had been subjected to such a disgustingly classic "girl thing." I should have known even then that guys don't invent names for things like, "doily." The Lone Ranger would never be heard saying to Tonto, "I can hardly wait to get back to camp and finish crocheting that doily."

Repentance Accomplished and Grandma Forgiven ~

In any case, I eventually repented for allowing that devastating assault on my budding masculinity and promised that from then on, I would only handle hooks that go on the end of fishing lines. I quietly slipped the painful episode into the category of things you never admit and sealed my newfound manliness by going outside, throwing a few rocks at a toad frog, and spitting on a couple of bugs.

I am violating my earlier vow not to divulge my breach of manhood for two reasons. In the first place, I don't worry so much about what people think anymore. I'm approaching that season of life where if you mention your childhood, people zone out because they begin to equate it with things like the Civil War. The more relevant factor is that there seems to be an interesting connection between crocheting and the media circus confronting us daily—a "common thread," if you will.

Doilies Look Different than Balls of String ~

The fact that crocheted items are handmade products is so obvious, it never gets questioned or even mentioned. When someone shows off a crocheted doily, for instance, nobody says, "My, what an interesting little wad of cotton," or "How clever—a bunch of different-sized holes tied together with a string." No, they exclaim things like, "Oh, what a beautiful piece—did you make it?" Conversely, if we show someone a ball of colored string, they don't begin to gush over it and ask if we made it ourselves. Most of us have sense enough to know one from the other—but what if the product being presented is made of a different kind of string?

Faithful Witnesses or Verbal Artisans?

Suppose the raw material is a string of words and events, and the "crochet hook" involved is the latitude to twist and loop them at will. Then the resulting product can be a dangerous distortion of the original material. With a ball of cotton string, the product may be a doily—but with a string of words and events, it's a "narrative."

If the issues of the day were seen as a ball of string, the task of those whose job it is to expose them to those who haven't had the opportunity to see them directly, would be to simply describe the "ball of string" for what it actually is, and to do that as clearly and honestly as possible. Unfortunately the temptation to rise above such simplicity can be overwhelming, and evidence of that abounds in our own culture and around the world. Reporters have in some cases become artisans, expert in the craft of verbal crochet and loathe to present a ball of string as merely a ball of string. Some seem to compulsively apply their editorial hook to the endless string of words and events unfolding around us daily. They twist and loop and tie them together until they are transformed into some kind of agenda-driven narrative—an ideological verbal "doily" that distorts and distracts attention away from the raw material from which it was manufactured.

Not a Modern Invention ~

Crocheting is an old art form whether with cotton or linen, like Grandma did it, or with strings of words and events. Sometimes malicious thoughts guide the media artisans just as the image of the doily in Grandma's mind guided her, and neither process is a modern invention. David dealt with it too. His enemies were busily attempting to "crochet" his words and actions into a hangman's noose. *All day they twist my words,* he said. *All their thoughts are against me for evil* (Psalm 56:5-6). Sound familiar?

And it isn't always about politics. Peter revealed that those who didn't like the content of Paul's writings were applying their editorial crochet hooks and twisting them into attractive doctrinal "doilies" to suit their sinful proclivities.

Peter said of them, *Untaught and unstable people twist* [Paul's words] *to their own destruction, as they do also the rest of the Scriptures* (2 Peter 3:16). Then he inserted this very relevant admonition, which is the point for us today:

> *You therefore, beloved, since you know this beforehand, beware lest you also fall from your own steadfastness, being led away with the error* [clever doctrinal doilies or political narratives] *of the wicked; but grow in the grace and knowledge of our Lord and Savior Jesus Christ.* (2 Peter 3:17-18)

Crocheted Doctrines and Eternal Consequences ~

When verbal artisans present a new "doily," they want our attention to be captivated by the skillful narrative they've created, so that we don't focus on the material from which it was fabricated. Perception is a powerful thing, and truth can be lost when the editorial crochet hooks go to work.

There's a funny thing about crocheted stuff that we all ought to remember. No matter how impressive it looks, if you find and untie the right knot, the whole thing will unravel until all that's left is the piece of string you started with. After all, it's just a bunch of holes tied together anyway.

Part IV
Right Side Up Revelations from Life's Impromptu Lessons

Introduction: Random Reflections on Some of Life's Teachable Moments

Has God ever done or said something in your life, and you thought your head would explode from the power of it? Long before I knew that the Holy Spirit existed, God brought experiences and incidents into my life that had virtually no significant impact on me or my view of the world at the time, but decades later, some of them began to emerge with an impact that was life-changing.

For instance, I learned some Greek words about forgiveness in a seminary classroom, and I read comments about it that were offered by an array of noteworthy scholars. I heard well-crafted expository messages from passages that dealt with it, and I even sang songs extolling its benefits, but that's not how I learned about forgiveness.

I began to learn about forgiveness as my heart crumbled inside of me when the weight of my sin hit it with the force of a sledgehammer. I learned about what forgiveness means in the midst of bitter tears, anguish of soul, and the desperation that attends just and unavoidable condemnation. Forgiveness had meaning when the One most damaged by failures I couldn't undo, displayed a love I will never understand and absorbed all the pain and loss as though the penalties were His. God designed all the intricate components that make forgiveness work, but life taught me what it *means*.

All of us have been invited to enroll as students in a course we might call, *"Life According to Jesus."* Having the Son of God walk "with" us in life is a source of inexpressible hope, but living life "through" Him adds a whole new dimension and constitutes a partnership that has the potential to redeem lives, restore relationships, revive churches, and transform cultures.

Jesus was not just *a* master teacher. He was *the* Master Teacher. His classroom traveled with Him and He was always at work. His presentations were likely to take place at any point throughout the day. The Word of God was all the source material He needed, and our hopelessness to understand life's mysteries or experience its greatest joys without it was His only rationale. He dealt directly with life's greatest questions, and the world around Him was an inexhaustible repository for illustrative material.

The wonderful truth is that His return to Heaven did not put an end to His teaching ministry, because as promised, He sent His Spirit to indwell every one of His followers and continue the teaching ministry He began. Through the Holy Spirit, He imparts truth designed not only to enrich our own lives, but to empower and direct us as change agents in the lives of others.

John referred to our personal relationship with the Holy Spirit as an "anointing" and described it as more than some kind of religious credentialing. He said:

> *These things I have written to you concerning those who try to deceive you. But the anointing which you have received from Him abides in you, and you do not need that anyone teach you; but as the same anointing teaches you concerning all things, and is true, and is not a lie, and just as it has taught you, you will abide in Him.* (1 John 2:26-27)

The Holy Spirit's activity in our lives is not constrained within the boundaries of a church service or a Christian music concert.

He's likely to unfold one of God's lesson plans anywhere. Some specific element of His truth could suddenly come to light while we're putting eggs in our shopping cart at the grocery store, or while we're maneuvering through traffic, or after waking out of a sound sleep in the middle of the night. Part of the adventure of learning from Him is the realization that He is sovereign over what we need to learn, and when, and what material needs to be involved in the process. That means that another step in perfecting His design in us could be about to begin at any point. Our task is to stay engaged, to pay attention, to respond when prompted, and to apply the principle as instructed.

My hope is that the Holy Spirit of God who delights to teach incomprehensible truth to undeserving people like me, will use the vignettes included here to be an encouragement, and that those who visit these pages will look more intently for His next unforgettable lesson.

Hope: $2.98, Plus Shipping & Handling

Living in the age of Amazon is pretty cool. Our first membership to Amazon Prime was a gift from our kids, and it reminded me of my introduction to pizza as a teenager. One little taste of pizza and I was ruined. It rendered a death sentence to any thought of Friday nights without it and moved pizza deprivation into the category of diagnosable dietary disorders.

Amazon Prime had a similar impact. Something had to be dreadfully wrong with folks who would climb into their car and risk a road rage-related cardiac event or death-by-vehicular-lunacy to go across town and buy something when just a few keystrokes could have it sitting on their front porch in a couple of days. For me, Amazon Prime was like fifty flavors of wonderful and such a radical contrast to my first mail order experience.

An Astonishing New World ~

My discovery that the US Postal Service could open doors to a world of wondrous delights began the day my brother bought a novelty catalog off the comic book rack at the drugstore for ten cents. It was full of the most compelling and desirable stuff I had ever seen, stuff you couldn't get anywhere else, at least nowhere I'd ever been. There were pictures and descriptions of incredible things I didn't even know existed, like itching powder, magic disappearing ink, a pen with a secret telescope, "whoopee" cushions, stink bombs, plastic imitation puke, and x-ray glasses. But all that was just kid stuff compared to the one thing that sent adrenaline coursing through my whole body—a pocket-sized, fully operational, super-secret spy camera—complete with two tiny rolls of film.

This amazing device represented heretofore unimagined opportunities to astonish my friends, embarrass my family, further alienate the neighbors, and finally get back at that crabby old Mrs. Watson who always talked about how fat I was getting. This super-secret spy camera would establish me as a sneaky force to be reckoned with, but such power does not come cheap. At a whopping $2.98, plus another $.50 for shipping and handling, it was one of the more expensive items in the catalog, but the ad claimed "guaranteed performance" and "precision construction." Who could ask for more?

Chronological Torture Begins ~

My lone revenue stream at that point was a weekly allowance of $.50, part of which my brother invariably managed to borrow before the coins got warm in my hand, so I had no reserves. But if I cut my brother off, I could accumulate the funds needed in a mere seven weeks. "Seven weeks" was easy to say, but it soon began to feel like torture. Mom didn't offer credit terms, and my brother was always broke, so I had no choice but to wait.

The weeks eventually crawled by, and my heart pounded as I sat at the kitchen table with my entire net worth in one hand and the order blank in the other. I laid three precious $1 bills on a sheet of notebook paper and carefully taped the forty-eight cents to the paper so they wouldn't rattle around and tempt the postal workers to steal. I slipped it in an envelope, licked the flap, applied the stamps, and ran down the lane to the mailbox. I was breathless with excitement as I closed the door and pulled the flag up to alert the postman that there was outgoing mail in the box.

Patience—Just More Torture ~

Mom said I had to be patient, and I was pretty good at it for the first couple of days, figuring it would take a day for the order to get wherever it was going and another day or so to get it back. By the third day, I was all done with the whole patience thing. I would run to the mailbox every day as soon as I got home, pull open the door and look inside, expecting to see a package with my name on it. Every day that I didn't get it was awful, but I would console myself with the hope that it would come the next day.

Nearly seven weeks dragged by—forty-seven days of running to the mailbox, breathlessly expecting that day to be the day, followed by forty-seven slow walks back to the house with nothing. But the forty-eighth trip was different. I can still recall the overwhelming joy of running back home, clutching that little package in my hand, not knowing until decades later that God would take my $2.98 plus shipping and handling and use it to send me something priceless. The only discernible image my super-secret spy camera was destined ever to deliver was an unforgettable picture of the difference between wishing for something and having hope with a valid basis.

The Picture Gets Developed ~

I was good at looking at things in that novelty catalog and wishing for them and did it for hours. I could look at that ad for itching powder and get lost in the thought of sprinkling some of it into my cousin's underwear. I could imagine my mom screaming when she discovered the fake puke on that chair she didn't let us kids sit on. It was fun to imagine those things and to wish I had them. The catalog was full of things to wish for, and wishes were free. I could have as many wishes as I wanted, but I never ran to the mailbox looking for anything because I had a wish for it.

Hope was different. Hope didn't come from just looking at the catalog. Hope was born out of my active response to what was offered, not some passive wish that it would magically come to me. Hope began with the awareness that something desirable was available and knowing what was required to have it.

> Hope is born out of an active response to what is offered.

Hope had a price. Unless and until the purchase price was paid, all that was available to me was just another empty wish. But when I slipped the money and the order form inside and sealed the envelope, hope began to stir. When I licked the stamp, hope grew. When the postman took my envelope out of the mailbox and drove off with it, hope exploded into living reality. Maybe I didn't own the camera yet, but I sure owned the hope of possessing it. It was mine, as much a commodity to me as the thing I had ordered. That camera was coming, and I was as confident that it was mine as if I had it in my hand. If it didn't come today, then maybe it would be here tomorrow.

A Hope, or Just Another Empty Wish?

So many people tell me that they "hope" they go to heaven. Having owned a super-secret spy camera and seen a picture of the difference between wishing and really having hope, I'm curious to know which one they have. Wishes are easy. They cost nothing, but they offer nothing. In a world accustomed to empty religious wishes, Paul encouraged us with this: *May the God of hope fill you with all joy and peace in believing, that you may abound in hope* (Romans 15:13a).

Having a ticket to heaven doesn't cost money, but it requires sacrifice and surrender. Meeting those requirements gives us a solid hope. Wishes may feel good for the moment, but hope will keep you running to the mailbox every day. Jesus promised He'd come for us, and if He doesn't come today, that's okay. We'll look again tomorrow.

No Audition Necessary

When you're seventeen, finding almost anything about yourself that looks like it might be an asset is a good thing. Regardless of whether it's something you developed on purpose or not, if having it helped to mask your insecurities and coax your self-esteem out of its usual place in the basement corner, it was to be treasured.

Impressive Notoriety ~

I found such a treasure. I discovered that I could take my right hand and push the index finger of my left hand backward until my fingertip touched the back of that same hand. As you would expect, it was recognized right off as an exceptionally cool thing to do—except for some girls, who would screw up their faces and ask stupid questions like, "Why would you want to do that?" Some of the guys thought I might be an alien, and let's face it, you just don't get much better stuff said about you than that.

Not every personal discovery at that point in my life turned out to be the kind of social accelerant that bending my finger backwards was. I liked reading, for instance, which was generally okay, I guess, until I discovered that I liked reading Shakespeare. An assignment in English started the whole thing. Forced exposure to that first play unearthed some inherited family defect in me that made all that Elizabethan English sound incredibly fascinating. I didn't mean to like it, but I did. I quietly checked out and read the school library's entire Shakespeare collection, being very careful not to risk social suicide by ever mentioning it to anyone—but there was a danger I didn't foresee.

Unmasked by "Loose Lips Lucy" ~

I was basically trusting of adults at that age, and I don't recall ever thinking of librarians in general as being evil. You'd think a librarian would represent the soul of discretion, especially one who noticed something as potentially destructive to a guy's life as liking Shakespeare. You'd think she would keep it to herself, or only bring it up in conversations outside of school, and at least 300 miles away, and with people who don't know you. No such consideration was forthcoming from "Loose Lips Lucy," the librarian. She inflicted an image adjustment on me that bending my finger into a square knot couldn't have overcome.

Her unrestrained excitement over my Shakespeare affliction led her to leak the information to my English teacher, and who knows how many others. My vision of the future was reduced to a barren wasteland that stretched out forever, or at least until graduation. But God's grace intervened in a way I never expected.

Birth and Death of a Stage Career ~

The English Department decided to bring Shakespeare's *Macbeth* to life on our own high school stage for the spring theatrical event. Let's just say that my name came up. My career as an actor blossomed that spring. It unfurled into the zenith of its glory, and faded into oblivion in the course of three productions on that stage. I discovered new definitions of "Shakespearean tragedy" in that process, but also that there is something strangely compelling about the whole "actor" thing.

Everyone fantasizes at times about being someone other than who they really are, someone radically different, someone more exciting, more accomplished, more revered—more loved. Actors get to do all that, to actually *be* that other person. Well ... okay, that's not quite accurate, is it? They don't really get to *be* the imaginary character. Pretending to be physically and emotionally involved in the lifestyles of those they portray is as close as they get. The actors themselves are real, but everything they present is illusion. We know that, yet we're drawn to it, and to them, anyway.

The Compelling Allure of the Stage ~

Actors seem to have the freedom to change themselves with none of the downsides. They get to be the hero or the heroine without assuming any of the risks they would face if their pretended situations were even remotely real. Actors get to defend the innocent, punish the guilty, rescue the captives, and save the world.

We covet the idea of a world where our actions do not have attendant consequences, even though we know in our hearts that such a world doesn't exist. We cherish the idea of being someone else, without having to really "be" someone else, and therein lies an irritating truth. Actors and actresses must at some point exit the stage, because acting is temporary. Eventually, the last line of the script must be delivered. Then the curtains come down. Then the cameras stop. Lights go off, costumes are discarded, and the makeup that hid all those defects finds its way down some bathroom drain. What awaits them then—a life of waiting for another script, another mask, another stage, and another curtain to hide behind?

The "Actors' Guild" of Jesus' Day ~

The hypocritical religious leadership of Jesus' day could have passed as a kind of "actors' guild." They were great at pretense and loved giving performances to admiring audiences, but they were something else altogether underneath their holy costumes. The life Jesus demonstrated and called people to follow was a threat to them and incited their continuous and eventually violent opposition.

The Pharisees were plagued by the same underlying problem confronting actors in any age. The life they portray can't really be lived except in brief little excerpts on a stage. In spite of that, the life of an actor is powerfully compelling because it seems to offer so much—so much freedom, so many privileges, so much attention, so much money, and so much pleasure. And perhaps the most seductive of all—so many ways to hide who they really are and what they're like on the inside.

A Life with No Pretense ~

Jesus called us to abandon our pretenses and live life as it really is, to be the person we really are. Our fantasies can never compete with life the way God intended it—to have romance with all its uncertainties, love with all its pain, danger with all its risks, courage with all its fears, and rainbows with all their stormy backgrounds. Jesus contrasted Himself with those who come only to take from us. He said, *The thief does not come except to steal, and to kill, and to destroy. I have come that they may have life, and that they may have it more abundantly* (John 10:10).

From the agonizing reality of a cross, and bearing all our failures and weaknesses, Jesus invites us to something greater than any actor's role. He offers a life that can really be lived, a stage that has no curtain, an audience that fills the world, and a story that never ends. He offers us the glory of today without a mask, and tomorrow without a script. No audition necessary.

Breaking Free from Two-Dimensional Christianity

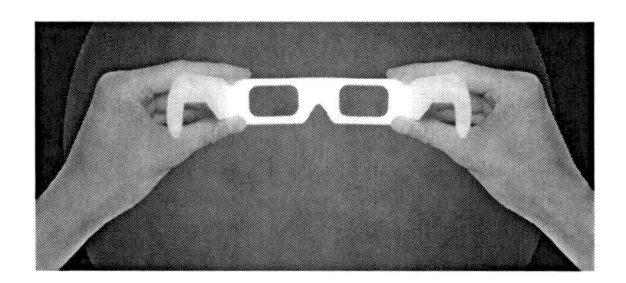

First-time experiences stick in your mind, don't they? I had one of them at the movies when I was fourteen—and, no, it didn't involve a girl, and it didn't involve lip contact with anything they didn't sell at the concession counter. It didn't make the "first time" category because I had never been to the movies, either. At my age, that would be ridiculous.

I was pushing fifteen, and we were entering the 1960s. My buddies and I had been going to movies since we were kids and had been thoroughly initiated into the rapidly expanding world of cinematic expression. We considered ourselves to be above average, sophisticated movie-goers, having sampled the full range of culturally relevant video genre—westerns, war movies, and horror flicks.

We were well-rounded supporters of all those important categories, but battle-hardened veterans when it came to the second most challenging genre of movie going for fourteen-year-olds—horror flicks. First place belonged, of course, to that collection of movies with the most consistently disgusting and hard to watch scenes, the dreaded "romance" category. We didn't think they deserved classification. We considered them to be just another pathetic and unappealing variety of horror movies that might have had possibilities with a little creative work. If one of the lovers had been zapped with some plutonium and their lips became a radioactive mutation that could suck the other's guts out, they might have been worth seeing, but that's a whole other discussion.

Horror Hits New Heights ~

Regardless, at this point in our careers, our adrenaline glands and cardiovascular systems had survived such paralyzing attacks as *Frankenstein*, *The Bride of Frankenstein*, *Frankenstein Meets the Wolfman*, and *Frankenstein Meets Igor's Mother-In-Law* (title may be a little off, but you get the idea). But tonight was going to be different. Tonight, Hollywood had promised horror at a whole new level. Tonight, the darkened theater would be transformed into the *House on Haunted Hill*.

This sounded scary, and we didn't know exactly what to expect, but still, we were veterans with a reputation to protect, and backing down was not an option. We had faced Hollywood's worst, and we wore our hard-earned bravado right up to the ticket window. We looked that ticket girl right in the eye as she tore off our tickets and said mechanically, "Thanks—now get your glasses out of that box over there." Glasses? What glasses??

Seeing Things Differently ~

The nervous apprehension was already starting. We didn't need paper glasses with red and green cellophane to watch Frankenstein go one-on-one with the Wolfman, but this was *House on Haunted Hill*, and this wasn't just horror—this was horror in 3-D. The assortment of macabre creatures lurking inside that creepy old house weren't going to be content to just wait for the usual collection of teenage idiots to cross their threshold tonight. Tonight, they were going to break free from the confines of the silver screen and burst right out into the audience and shove their drooling, bloodthirsty ugliness right in front of our faces. This 3-D stuff was going to be serious.

Well, I'm not fourteen anymore (as you probably suspected), but I'm still captivated by the visual phenomenon of 3-D. Though we live and move in a three-dimensional world, most of us don't consider the concept beyond the commonplace physical realities that are associated with it.

The apostle Paul thought about it, though, and even inserted the idea in the midst of a prayer as he pleaded with God on behalf of his beloved Ephesian believers. Paul wanted them to experience a personal intimacy and involvement with Jesus Christ that extended beyond superficial rituals and empty clichés.

Jesus in 3-D ~

Paul knew that when robbed of deeper internal realities, those external trappings can obscure and obstruct the power of God's transcendent truth. His request was that they would come to know *what is the width and length and depth and height—to know the love of Christ which passes knowledge* (Ephesians 3:18-19).

Three-dimensional love—imagine that! No wonder he was quick to say that such love passes knowledge. That kind of love is beyond the two dimensions of just the physical and mental. It has depth—another dimension altogether.

Paul's prayer reflects two truths—the love of Christ is needed to give the Christian life its proper "depth," its three-dimensional reality; and without that love, the Church is only an illusion of what God intended it to be.

My buddies and I did survive the *House on Haunted Hill*. In spite of all that 3-D hype, none of those malicious creatures ever left the screen that night. It was all just a clever deception, fooling our eyes and minds to make it look like they did. Nothing was really three-dimensional in that theater except us and the stuff around us.

Nothing about the love of Christ is hype or illusion. It's true 3-D. Knowing the real, deep, and life-changing love of Christ creates and sustains a three-dimensional reality that is eternal, energized, empowered, and satisfying.

Is God's Real Name "Harvey"?

James Stewart played the leading role in the 1950 movie adaptation of a Pulitzer Prize winning play written by Mary Chase called *Harvey*. The story was based on a man's relationship with an imaginary, six-foot-tall rabbit named Harvey. The rabbit was Elwood's constant companion and a trusted friend with whom he interacted regularly and whose counsel proved more trustworthy than the advice proffered by most of his human counterparts. The obvious problem was that Harvey didn't exist, or maybe it was that he did, only not in a way that most folks would have been comfortable with. In any case, it was a very popular movie back in those days, and the pros and cons of imaginary friends got a lot of discussion from movie-goers in the '50s, and in some ways, the core questions still linger today.

A Bigger Problem ~

Of course, in today's world, nobody's concerned about the existence of giant, invisible, woodland creatures with human personalities and characteristics unless you work in a psych ward, or happen to indulge in mood-altering substances. The very real quandary we face today centers on a character much bigger than a 6' 3½" rabbit, but who happens to share Harvey's challenging features of being invisible and inaudible, at least in the normally accepted meaning of those terms.

Sometimes I think we should just invite Mary Chase's perspective into our next discussion about God. How about beginning with an opening question like this: "Is God's real name Harvey?" After all, the response often encountered by those who claim to have a functioning relationship with God is not unlike that of her character in the story.

Familiar Responses ~

The more benevolent observers of the story's main character, Elwood, thought of him as just being a little "off," a few nuts short of a fruit cake, you might say. To them, he was simply a sad but benign mental case who should be tolerated, maybe pitied, but never taken seriously. Those who were less compassionate were uneasy around him and considered him to be dangerously irrational, unpredictable, and potentially threatening. They were convinced that for the protection of the general population, and for his own good, Elwood should have his movements restricted, that he should be confined and isolated to the company of others like himself, and of course, carefully supervised at all times.

These attitudes are not unfamiliar, are they? They are mirrored in the words and actions of many in America these days that are directed toward evangelical Christianity. To the vast majority of those who represent mainstream media, entertainment, and academia, those of us who are followers of Jesus are all just another version of Elwood.

A Question of Reality ~

In the story, it's interesting to note that the value of any guidance or advice that Harvey allegedly provided to Elwood was predicated upon the question of his existence. Elwood had only the testimony of his personal experience to offer as proof of Harvey's reality, and as far as his critics were concerned, that was not enough. The general conclusion was that since Harvey didn't really exist, all those things credited to Harvey either didn't happen at all and were simply fabricated to help make Harvey look real, or if they were done at all, they were actually done by Elwood himself.

Others might argue philosophically that since Harvey clearly existed in Elwood's mind, then he did, in fact, exist because Elwood had "created" him. That conclusion isn't unfamiliar either, is it? The same premise is postulated frequently in our day with regard to the existence of the God we serve and our relationship with Him. That view doesn't deny the "existence" of God, per se, but relegates Him, His characteristics, His power, and His entire kingdom to the confines of our mind. Those holding that view declare that God only exists because we have chosen to believe that He does, that He is simply a made-up entity to help us get through tough times and avoid dealing with life's incomprehensible difficulties and insoluble mysteries. Multitudes hold that opinion and openly declare it.

One of two possibilities must be true of God, and the implications of each are huge. Either God actually exists, and He created me, or He does not exist, and I have simply "created" Him. If He created me, then I am, by definition, His. In that case, I am inherently subject to His authority, evaluated according to His standards, dependent upon His provision, and ultimately accountable to Him.

Realities and Implications ~

If, on the other hand, I created Him, then He is nothing more than my personal and private hallucination. Any set of standards He might claim, and any authority to enforce them is subject to my approval, and constrained within the flexible boundaries of my own desires, whims, and preferences. His power to provide is subjugated to the extent of my own personal talents, abilities, and intellect. If He is not God, but only "god," then he is no longer invisible, nor inaudible. I see him in the mirror every day, and I hear him in the tones of my own proud declarations of what I will or will not do. If he is not God, but only god, then I am accountable to no one but myself.

Mary Chase was not the first to create a *Harvey*, nor will she be the last. The truth is that we humans have created a whole menagerie of invisible creatures to interact with, and we've been doing it for eons of time. The sons of Israel, for instance, apparently thought they needed something extra when they ran into some challenges after leaving Egypt. Their preference was to go with something more imposing to converse with than a giant rabbit. They opted for a huge bull and were so convinced of his existence that they made a statue of him. Sadly for them, their god, like all created gods, couldn't produce when the chips were down. The question remains, though. Does God exist only because I choose to believe that He does? Does my *faith*, my capacity to believe, establish His only reality, or is there something else to consider?

Harvey—Always Just a Rabbit ~

Harvey was always a rabbit, never a man. Conversely, Elwood would never become anything like a rabbit, with a twitchy nose and huge floppy ears. The God who "is" forbade any attempt to make anything that we declare to be an image of Him. The only "image" of Him that exists is us. We are His image, and He revealed Himself by becoming one *of* us and one *with* us who believe in Him.

> God became one *of* us and one *with* us who believe in Him.
> ~

Harvey never revealed himself at all. He never inspired a book, never delivered a public address, and never subjugated the "laws" of nature to his will. Harvey never spoke hope to the hopeless, never healed the incurable, never freed anyone from bondage, and never condensed the wisdom of the ages into simple statements so profound that libraries can't contain the books attempting to expound on them. Harvey never offered to abolish Elwood's failures or to take every disgusting, repulsive thing Elwood ever did upon himself and die in his place.

Jesus isn't a figment of anyone's imagination, and He doesn't hide His speech, or obscure His presence, or disguise His identity. He isn't real because we believe. We believe because He *is* real … undeniably real. Apart from Him, all you have left is *Harvey*.

Love Those Hoverboards

I feel compelled to react to the question that's on everybody's mind these days. Why do those "hoverboard" scooters keep catching on fire, and what are the spiritual implications?

Well, OK ... so maybe it's not on your mind all that much, but I'm having a struggle. In spite of skillfully avoiding anything that had the word "organic" on the label, and refusing to even look at the "healthy choices" on any menu, I somehow managed to survive another year, which means that I'm stuck here again, a writer on the threshold of yet another Valentine's Day. The annual invasion of love themes has arrived in full force, and is forming itself into the familiar vortex that reaches out like a *Star Trek* tractor beam, determined to suck in every Tom, Dick, and Harriett with a keyboard.

I figured somebody should prove that there's at least one of us capable of producing something in February that doesn't involve a romantic fantasy. I knew that resistance would be tough. Little heart-shaped boxes of candy start popping up like toadstools in the yard after a summer rain this time of year, accompanied, of course, by the inevitable barrage of seductive ads for intimate things guys can order online, so they don't have to actually go anywhere, or think. And there's no way to dodge the tsunami of sappy greeting cards within easy reach of every check-out line.

Cupid's arrows are flying around like election year campaign promises, and every guy knows that Cupid's arrows this time of year are not nice. They're tipped with guilt-inducing warheads, designed to make us feel like crude emotional Neanderthals if we don't get on board. My plan was to deal with all that love stuff like I do the existence of IRS auditors—can't stop them from being in the world, but determined to avoid any risk of personal contact. So, lo and behold, the vital issue of explosive hoverboards presents itself, and offers a glimpse of one of God's favorite subjects without pandering to another Hallmark holiday.

The innovative design for these new scooters achieved almost instant popularity when they were introduced, and stores had trouble keeping their inventories on pace with their sales. Unfortunately, it wasn't long before reports began to emerge that the devices were catching fire and even exploding. Apparently, the major problems were not with the original versions, but mainly confined to the knockoffs. The cheaper imitations looked flawless on the surface, and in the beginning, performed just like the originals. The problems lay hidden underneath, lurking in the flawed components inside. The design itself was field-tested and sound, but the weaker, substandard quality of the material used in their construction doomed the imitations to eventual failure. There was never a question whether disaster awaited them; it was only a matter of how soon it would happen, and how severe the damage would be.

God doesn't make scooters, but He is an inventor. He's the Designer and Chief Engineer of human relationships, and marriage, that consummate expression of love between a man and a woman, is His flagship achievement. It is so significant that He used it to describe the nature of the relationship between Jesus Christ and all who follow Him. But if we look at the status of God's premier product in our land, we might find some similarities with the knockoff hoverboards.

> God is the Designer and Chief Engineer of human relationships.

Marriage can certainly be complex, and there are lots of components involved, but one stands out as absolutely vital. God made love indispensable. He said that without love, nothing we do for Him is of any value at all, and if it's irreplaceable in the greater relationship, it is no less vital in the one designed to illustrate it. Like any good designer, God chose the materials needed for marriage in consideration of the kinds of stresses and pressures it would be subjected to. There's a reason, after all, that we don't make hammers out of glass. The intensity of the pressures married couples would face demanded that the love involved be of the highest quality available. That can be problematic. Higher quality things are always more scarce, costly, and difficult to obtain, adding patience and sacrifice to the price. No wonder it gets so tempting to slip in cheap, unreliable substitutes, and grab what benefit you can until it all falls apart.

Building a relationship around Hollywood's flimsy, self-centered exercise in mutual manipulation instead of the sacrificial, other-centered love that God ordained, results in the same effect that the substandard parts are having on the hoverboards. After a while, the flaws show up and the friction burns the life out of its major working part. The fun is over, and what's left is headed for the trash bin.

Nearly half of all the marriages that will take place in America this year won't make it, and it's not a fault of the design. It's the flimsy, cheap, and unreliable material in the major component that will doom them. Abandoning the deep, sacrificial devotion that God ordained in search of a passing and superficial Hallmark moment gains only a legacy of failure.

All hoverboards have batteries that run down, at which point the fun stops for a while. Marriages do that, too—not surprising that in both cases, the ones built with the right stuff inside can be recharged again and again, while the cheap imitations explode.

On second thought, maybe Valentine's Day isn't so bad. Everybody's relationship needs a little recharge once in a while, even if it involves a heart-shaped box of candy and a sappy card.

*This is My commandment,
that you love one another as I have loved you.*
John 15:12

Dynamite: The Power Is in What It Does, Not in What It's Called

"Dynamite" was a peculiar dog with whom I shared life for a while as a kid. He was mostly German Shepherd, but I suspected he might be part possum because he was slow, lazy, and after every meal, he demonstrated an ability to lie down and play dead better than any possum I ever saw.

One Saturday afternoon Dynamite was doing his possum impersonation while a buddy and I sat under a tree discussing whether or not the fish might be biting, and whether there was any dependable way to know that, short of having to dig worms and hike down to the creek. We sat there staring at Dynamite like subjects in a hypnosis sideshow while we pondered the whole fishing enigma, including whether the bony little creatures were even worth the time and effort to catch them anyway.

My friend broke the silence and jerked us in a totally unrelated direction. Without looking up, he drawled, "D'you reckon that Dynamite knows he's a dog?" My focused investigation of the relevant issues—the best place to find worms and the questionable value of bony little fish—was instantly ruined. I frowned at the pointless intrusion and said, "That's ridiculous. Why in the world would you ask a stupid question like that, anyway?" "Well," he said, "does he?" "Don't be an idiot," I shot back, "of course he does." "And just how do you figure that?" he demanded. "Well," I explained, "he obviously knows he's a dog because, a) he barks once in a while when he feels like it, b) he always growls at the cat, and c) he eats *dog* food. Would he be doing any of that if he thought he was a goat?"

My succinct assessment was impressive enough to remove the subject from further debate, and if Dynamite did have any noteworthy insights regarding his status in the animal kingdom, or his skill in doing possum impersonations, he kept them to himself. In any case, I don't recall catching any fish that afternoon.

Our less than scientific exchange back then at least highlights this simple truth. Of all God's creatures, we humans are the only ones stepping up to boldly assert that we have figured out who and what we are. We've demonstrated an obsession with classifying things (including ourselves) and can't rest until we categorize everything we find that crawls, runs, slithers, creeps, flies, and hops around us. We may not even know what most of them are called, but whatever they are, we remain fairly confident that we aren't one of them—with the possible exception of a woman I read about recently who thinks she might actually be a cat.

We feel a bit uncomfortable until we know what things are and where they fit. During a hospital visit in the early days of my ministry, I offered to pray with a man I just met. "Are you a Christian?" he asked, and I replied that I was. He then wanted to know just what kind of Christian I was. "Baptist," I said. "Oh," he responded. "What kind of Baptist? Are you Northern Baptist? Southern Baptist? Missionary Baptist? Free Will Baptist? Hardshell Baptist…what?" "Independent," I replied. "Independent from what?" he asked. "I guess independent from anybody that isn't us," I said. "Why do you need to know all that?" "Oh," he said, "I just wanted to clarify what you're trying to turn me into."

The expanding array of names, titles, creeds, and identifying standards we create in an attempt to define ourselves looks like a confusing linguistic kaleidoscope compared to the few words needed by the One we claim to be following. After announcing that He would soon be leaving them, Jesus said simply,

> *A new commandment I give to you, that you love one another; as I have loved you, that you also love one another. By this all will know that you are My disciples, if you have love for one another.* (John 13:34-35)

Our voluminous collection of creeds, statements, covenants, pledges, and declarations testifies to our obsessive desire for identity and recognition, and we reinforce them with certificates, rituals, garments, pins, and bumper stickers. Jesus, on the other hand, chose one profoundly simple standard, and it can't be signed with a pen, stuck on our car, or framed and hung on a wall. It is not a religious exercise to be done in specific surroundings with certain people on particular days, and it isn't a meaningless cliché we repeat. It is a personal replication of His own behavior toward us. That alone becomes the definitive characteristic of who we are, and it touches everything we do. The Lord Himself imparts it identically to all, but designed it to be dispensed in ways as uniquely individual as we are. It is universally applicable, culturally inclusive, eternally unchangeable, and dynamically transformational.

The identifying love He commanded is an unselfish, deeply felt, righteously expressed, and openly demonstrated commitment to the welfare of others, with no expectation beyond their benefit and the Father's approval. Its application alone will suffice to illustrate His nature, define His followers, and condemn every failed counterfeit. This grand "one another" phenomenon leaves no one untouched, no one left out, and none lifted up above others.

"Dynamite" was just my dog's name. It didn't really define him or even make him energetic, much less explosive. How tragic if that becomes true for any of us called "disciple."

Ambushed at Walmart

Phones these days are incredible. Mine has little "notification" beeps and tones built into it to alert me and tell me who's calling. That way, I get to prepare myself for the conversation, or decline it altogether. Maybe God should have made joy so that it comes with an advance beeper. Without it, people are vulnerable to having joy just sneak up and pounce on them without warning, and its impact can be extensive. Followers of Jesus are particularly at risk, and especially so around Christmas.

Let me illustrate. In spite of the wonders of Amazon and the internet, at times we're still faced with having to actually go inside a store during Christmas. I know … that fact alone is sobering enough, but it gets worse. Sometimes it involves Walmart—and on a weekend. Ducking in to grab an item is challenging enough at any point, but Walmart at Christmas is different. In our annual struggle to survive the snares of Christmas as redefined by Hallmark and Hollywood, it is one of those venues we try to avoid. In spite of that, I was forced to enter the lair of the retail giant in the midst of Christmas mania.

Not being a naïve first-timer, I prepared myself. I gathered up my spiritual armor, prayed for courage, double-checked the status of my smart phone batteries, and synched our "Evernote" lists. Walmart was a place for holiday warfare, not for serene "visions of sugar plums" and Christmas joy, so I headed out with resolute determination. My "anti-commercialized holiday" attitude was primed with a finely tuned critical spirit—a vital asset in approaching the battlefield itself.

My list of instantaneous judgments was locked and loaded, ready for the usual set of enemy combatants—oppressive crowds of insensitive shoppers jamming the aisles, people who park their cars crooked and take up extra spaces, and stock people who fail to put out enough of the main thing I'm going there to get. And complicating it even more was the disturbing awareness that my presence was supporting the materialism and commercialization of everything spiritual about Christmas. I could hear the voice of John the Baptist in my head yelling, "Hypocrite!" The combination condensed into my classic "Christmas shopping frown." It was etched into my countenance with a clarity that would have made Ebenezer Scrooge envious.

Making the trek from the hinder regions of the parking lot, my Christmas frown and I were busily reviewing a list of unforeseen disasters that could be lurking ahead, when a young mother heading back to her car caught my eye and interrupted my negative reverie. She had one of those baby carrying gizmos hanging from the crook in her arm with a little blanket thrown over it to protect her little treasure from the cold wind. I noticed right away that something wasn't quite right about her. Given the pervasive atmosphere of holiday urgency, she looked unreasonably relaxed, and her mood looked way too bright and happy. "She's just young and inexperienced," I concluded. "When she's older and more mature, she'll be able to exhibit a more appropriate aura of Walmart Christmas misery."

Just as I approached, she paused, lifted a corner of the blanket, and initiated a little peeping game with her baby. Tiny laughter rose from the warmth of the little carriage in response to the mother's smiling face and happy tones, and a totally unanticipated thing happened. With no warning at all, watching that random scene triggered something surprisingly powerful, and completely contradictory to everything else inside me at the time. It wasn't like a distinguishable memory or specific set of emotions—just an instant and overwhelming awareness of what a thousand little moments like that have meant to me over the years.

A sense of pure joy erupted right there in the middle of the Walmart parking lot. In spite of all the seasonal pressure, and the malicious irritations lurking inside the store, my carefully constructed "pre-Walmart entry" Christmas frown disintegrated on the spot. I lost all control of my "burdened shopper" persona, and almost laughed out loud.

See what I mean? I was totally unprepared—ambushed. That's why joy should come with warnings. It can make sudden, uncontrolled alterations to your whole point of view and dismantle all your defenses, and it's hard to shake when it happens. Inside the store, the crowd of Christmas shoppers was doing what Christmas shoppers do—dodging obstacles, grabbing potential purchases, fighting kids with Olympic skills at snatching impulse items, all the while trying to jockey their carts into a winning position in the checkout line. All that was normal and predictable, but that day it was noticeably less irritating than usual.

"Maybe," I thought, "that little mom has somehow affected the whole store." Then I noticed something else I hadn't really thought about before. The bustling crowd wasn't just a crowd anymore. They all had individual faces, and I was suddenly captivated by how unique they were. I looked from face to face and thought, "Every face in this crowd can say, 'He came to Bethlehem for me.'" The knowledge wasn't new, but the overwhelming awareness of the love involved was. We're not a crowd to Him. He didn't come to die for us in general, and every face is profoundly significant to Him.

> "Every face in this crowd can say, 'He came to Bethlehem for me.'"

On second thought, maybe it's better if joy sneaks up on us once in a while, especially if it screws up our well-prepared Grinch impersonations. A dose of Christmas joy hiding in a baby's laugh, and a fresh sense of wonder at God's love in the aisle at Walmart, might be a Christmas surprise we never forget.

For Mom: The Brightest Morning Ever

The Lord escorted my mother out of this world in early 2016 just prior to her ninety-second birthday and introduced her to that place He had gone to prepare for her so long ago. Reflecting on that event, and what that whole process means, unleashed a stampede of random memories and thoughts, but there were one or two that seemed worth sharing.

I remember standing at her bedside one evening, just looking down at Mom's little frame. Her eyes were closed, and her breathing was kind of shallow. Others had stepped out for some reason, and for a few minutes, there were just the two of us in the small hospital room. It was one of those "frozen in time" moments, silent except for the muffled sound of the air blowing through the heater vent.

A Sad and Blatant Contradiction ~

She was so small and frail now, so weak, so isolated, and in the world's value system, altogether irrelevant. Seeing her like this was such a contrast, and more than that, such a blatant contradiction of the vibrant, capable, strong, creative, and energetic woman who brought me into the world so many years ago and who had fought her way past more obstacles and endured more crises than I could ever recount.

I thought about where her journey had brought her in these recent months and how long and dark it had become. I stood there groping for some profound thing to say, some deeply moving insight to grab onto that would be worthy of the implications of this scene. All the most basic and vital realities of life and faith were unfolding before me, and at that moment, I had nothing. The only thought that stuck its head through the rubble right then was an irritating, out of place, clichéd adage. "It's always darkest just before the dawn." "Well," I thought, "it's certainly dark enough and has been for a long time, but I don't see much of a dawn right now."

Persistent Grace ~

In my younger days, we weren't "church people," at least not in the usual, evangelical, "Bible Belt" connotation of the term. We went to church on special occasions a few times a year but weren't members, and I wasn't a Sunday School kid by any stretch of the imagination. That wasn't noticeably bothersome to any of us, though, because not fitting in with the cultural patterns around us was not an uncommon characteristic for our family. After all, we were considered "Yankees," and blending in for an Ohio family transplanted into a tight-knit little southern Virginia community in the 1940s was going to have its limits. It didn't matter that Mom had lived here since she was a teenager, or that I was born in my grandmother's house three blocks from Main Street ... we had "northern accents" and didn't go to church. That made us outsiders, but in spite of our unchurched outsider status, the grace of God found its way to Mom, anyway.

At some point before I reached that age when girls somehow cease to be quite so disgusting, Mom began to listen to a radio preacher named Oliver B. Greene. His broadcast came on at some early hour, and it was Mom's "wake-up" system. She'd begin her day by lying there in the bed listening to him declare the love of God, and how she could have eternal life through faith in Christ. One morning, after hearing another of his daily appeals, she knelt beside her bed and gave her heart and life to the One who had given His for her. Mom was different after that. She didn't suddenly become perfect, as all of us who had intimate contact with her can attest, and she didn't become weirdly religious. But the faith she extended to Jesus Christ that day remained an indelible part of who she was from that time onward. And at this point, that single event in her life took precedence over everything.

> That single event took precedence over everything.

An Object Lesson in Values ~

Seeing her like she was that evening was an object lesson in values that I wish I had seen more clearly earlier in my life, and one that I wish I had applied more consistently throughout my life. The truth about the world's fraudulent claims of value and the sad misappropriation of life they cost were clearer than ever. After a lifetime of struggling to acquire enough of it to get by, money had nothing it could offer Mom anymore. She grew up in a household well acquainted with the lack of it as her family struggled through the kinds of financial hardships that were commonplace during The Great Depression. But it wouldn't matter to her tonight if she could swap bank accounts with Bill Gates, or if she had the kind of iconic popularity that would draw a crowd that would make Donald Trump envious. It would alter nothing.

Mom, like so many of us, spent so much of her life trying to gain or maintain some kind of control, and now the frail little person lying before me had lost personal control over almost everything. Dementia had taken away her capacity to make any significant decision. Age and disease had ravaged her physically and made her totally dependent for even the most basic care. *The only thing left that Mom had absolute, unchallenged, and unassailable ownership of was the promise she received from the lips of her risen Savior while kneeling beside another bed so many decades earlier.*

An Unassailable Promise ~

Age and disease might have taken control of her mind and body, but they couldn't take away her promise. Legal documents might have stripped her of the right to make important decisions, but they couldn't strip her of that promise. Every value system that the world had to offer was failing her right now, but her promise couldn't be touched by their collapse.

As I looked down through the tears and frustration of having nothing to offer her, I realized again that I wasn't the only one in the room looking down on her. The One who met with her in that other bedroom years ago was there, too. At that meeting, Mom wasn't destitute, but she relinquished everything to have Him. Now, when everything else was really gone, she was still His. The One who gave that promise to Mom back then, said quietly, but with absolute authority, *"I've got this. It's only dark a little longer. Then the dawn that's coming is like none she's ever seen. Your mom's going to wake to the brightest morning ever."*

Broken but Priceless

My brother and I crouched halfway down the stairs, hugging the balusters and barely breathing as we stared at the scene in the living room below. Had the picture been set to music, the crescendo would have erupted the moment when a beautiful new Lionel train came chugging from behind the tree. Powdery "smoke" puffed out of the locomotive's stack, and a distinctive whistle filled the room. I was breathless, paralyzed with a combination of excitement that it might actually be real and fear that it might somehow not be. A real Lionel train! I had only seen them behind the glass in department store windows, but there it was—in *our* house! Growing up, we didn't get many toys and didn't dare to dream of anything on the level of a Lionel train. I figured that things like that were beyond the level of any Christmas "goodness" that my brother and I could reach.

Another Christmas Birth ~

The birth of Christ may have been the central focus of our celebration, but that Christmas marked the birth of another love relationship for me. My love for trains, and for that train in particular, was born that morning. My grandpa was a railroad engineer, and trains were his means of providing for our family. He was the only dad I knew at the time, and Grandpa loved trains. He loved trains and I loved him, so loving trains was a natural. He almost never played with anything with us, but this train was different, and we spent hours together with it.

Life and growing up brought their inevitable changes, and the moving up, moving out, and moving on slowly eased the train into that category of treasured things you only take out and look at on rare occasions. Space constraints eventually forced it into a storeroom at my mom's house, which was fine until that awful day she decided to let my uncle's little boy (who could have been rented out to demolish buildings) "borrow" it. By the time I learned what she'd done, any rescue attempt was already months too late, and the train was reduced to a subject for sad reminiscing of tragic losses in melancholy moments at Christmas time.

Hopelessly Broken ~

Years later, I happened to be tasked with searching through old boxes of nondescript junk in my uncle's storage shed, and stumbled upon one that was worn and faded with age. I pulled the flaps back, and as the dim light began to unveil the contents of the box, my breath caught in my throat. Inside was what was left of my train. Unexpected tears found their way down my face as I looked at the broken remains. Wheels had been pulled off, cars were broken, tracks were bent. Parts and pieces were tangled together in a dusty, hopeless-looking wad. I folded the flaps back, picked up the old box, and just stood there and hugged it—feeling a deepening and unmistakable sense of kinship with the broken mess inside. Abuse had stripped it of everything and turned it into a worthless wreck, but its value to me had escaped unscathed.

> I hugged it—feeling a deepening and unmistakable sense of kinship with the broken mess inside.

I don't know how many calls I made or how many train shops I contacted during the years that followed, but their conclusions were the same. Repairs were impossible, and even if it could be fixed, it wasn't worth it—or so I was told. Then we discovered a little out-of-the-way train shop up in the mountains, and after much prodding, my hard-earned pessimism lost out to my wife's insistence that we could make it a fun trip, so we headed west.

Not Just Valuable—Priceless ~

The owner, a compassionate and avid collector, said if I'd leave it with him, he would see what he could do—no promises from him, no expectations from me. Months later, he called us and said we could pick it up, and off we went. He brought it from his workshop and gingerly placed the locomotive on a track on his counter. A nationwide network of Lionel collectors managed to find every broken and missing part, and it was like that Christmas all over again. "Take care of it," he said. "It's a valuable piece now." "It's more than that," I told him. "This train is priceless, but not because you restored it. It was just as priceless back when it was a broken worthless mess in a dusty cardboard box."

My train, restored and whole, has come to rest now, its journey through my life ending with the realization that it isn't the only thing in my house that was hopelessly broken, rejected, and lost, and then loved and restored. Someone loving the broken and useless, and seeing them as a treasure not for sale at any price, is what brought Jesus here. How fitting that I met my train on Christmas Day, and we ended up so much alike.

Parable in the Park

A few years ago, a little nine-year-old boy with autism was enjoying a warm, sunny afternoon at Battlefield Park with his family. It was one of those perfect fall afternoons in Virginia, but this one ignored their usual tendency to elude weekends and sneaked in on a Sunday. In the relaxing environment of a park full of potential distractions, it wasn't surprising that Robbie's parents had their attention drawn away for a moment. That brief moment of relaxation and escape for Robbie's parents soon became a source of awful regret, because it provided a doorway for their little guy to manage an escape of his own. A few independent and unobserved steps quickly took him out of their sight and transformed a beautiful day at the park into a nightmarish ordeal.

Shock and Alarm ~

Someone sent a frantic 911 call as the realization sank in that he was gone. Cell phones and social media quickly spread the alarm throughout the region that a handicapped little boy was lost and in danger. The usual first responders showed up right away and began the initial stages of the search. State and local police, fire departments, and other rescue personnel fanned out and began to comb the area, hoping, of course, that someone would catch sight of him quickly.

Tensions rose with the fading daylight, and more calls went out for help. Headlights from cars and trucks bringing more volunteers began to build levees of hope against the rising tide of fear and anxiety that came with the deepening shadows. Nocturnal creatures scurried in the leaves as darkness cloaked the woods and fields around the park, their usual routines wrecked by the beams of a small army of flashlights.

Hours morphed into days. Scores of volunteers became hundreds, dogs were brought in, helicopters took to the skies, and divers began to search the nearby river. Thousands waited and prayed, listening to updates and reports wherever they could find them, sharing their faith, bolstering hope however they could.

"Boots on the Ground" Compassion ~

This one lost little boy became a unifying force in the region. People took time off from work, abandoned their personal lives and schedules, and ignored increasing fatigue and discomfort as the weather turned colder. Volunteers from all backgrounds and all walks of life joined hearts and hands and took to the woods wanting no reward beyond finding him alive.

Each new day threatened the energy and optimism that everyone fought not to lose—two days passed, then three, then four. As the fifth day dawned, fears and anxieties were condensing around the local weather report. No one wanted to say it out loud, but everyone knew that if he wasn't found before that night, he wouldn't survive the cold and rain that were coming.

Faith and Hope Fade ~

By noon on Friday, day six, if hope existed at all, it was more like a stubborn determination not to quit than anything else—a refusal to give up the search, because to give up meant giving little Robbie up. For some in the group, the focus of their determination had shifted from finding him alive to just finding him. They wanted at least to bring his little body back and allow his family some measure of closure.

Beleaguered hope staggered under the increasing weight of each new forecast. The early winter storm and the sharp drop in temperature coming with it, were ahead of schedule, and would arrive by late afternoon.

Believers Refuse to Relinquish Hope ~

By Friday, any expectation of finding Robbie alive, or even finding him at all, was relegated to the realm of faith alone. No rethinking of strategies or rearranging of search patterns had any power left to give hope, and were abandoned in favor of God's words, like, *Call to Me, and I will answer you, and show you great and mighty things, which you do not know* (Jeremiah 33:3).

Around two o'clock that afternoon just as the cold rain began to fall in some parts of the area, a man who chose to remain anonymous finally caught a glimpse of Robbie's little body curled up in a dry creek bed near a quarry. He was clearly in need of medical attention, but he was alive. As the news spread, praises to God erupted like a volcano. Gratitude was palpable everywhere. Grim became glorious, and the spirit of celebration was overwhelming.

Joy Unrestrained ~

People who had never met Robbie hugged each other and cried. Grateful hands were raised heavenward by multitudes whether they participated directly in the search or not. Tears of joy flowed unrestrained from those whose hearts had been knit together for days with this lost little boy and his gripping story. The praise and worship were spontaneous and pervasive, and nothing artificial could have enhanced it. If any words were needed at all, "He once was lost, but now is found ..." would have sufficed beautifully.

Robbie's story gave me a fresh vision of what evangelism means. Robbie was not just another little kid. He was a very handicapped little kid. He didn't understand his situation, and didn't know why he was cold and miserable. He couldn't call out for help, or respond to those calling him. He didn't realize the danger he faced, much less how to avoid it. He had no way to know how to get home, and no grasp of what it meant to be lost. Someone had to find him or it was over. Yet God took all those things this little boy could not do and used them to unleash more selfless, sacrificial, heroic love than many of us had ever seen.

Maybe More than a Story ~

I thought at first that this was just a story about a lost little boy. Then I thought it might be a story about the power of love, compassion, and sacrifice. But maybe Robbie's story is bigger than that. Maybe the One who came to seek and to save those who are lost, wanted to give us another parable. Maybe He wanted to show us again how helpless the lost really are, and why they must be sought, and maybe He wanted us to feel the joy He feels when they are found.

Epilogue:
The Last Scene
~

Epilogue: The Last Scene

I always hated the last scene. On those rare Saturday afternoons as a child when I was lucky enough to be transported to the "wild west" via the marvel of cinema, I was always enraptured by the daring exploits of whatever cowboy hero was on display that week. The adrenalin was always in high gear for the climactic race against time. If the hero was to rescue the girl and save the town, he had to cut the bad guy off at the pass.

After a harrowing race, he would finally catch up, and at the last second, he would leap from his beautiful Palomino steed, knock the villain off his brand X brown horse, and together they would roll down the strategically selected hillside. Then, the hero would totally disable the bad guy with a single punch to the jaw, never losing his impressive white hat in the process. It was breathtaking and provided enough fuel for months of dreams and endless role playing with my cousin (who, by the way, never wanted to be the one on the brown horse). But then there was that awful last scene.

They never mentioned it directly, but it was clear in the last scene that the hero had been subjected to a bath and made to put on his "good clothes." His dusty, plaid "fighting" shirt was gone. Now he was sporting a freshly ironed one with embroidered doo-dads and little pearly buttons, and his everyday boots had been replaced with the shiny ones you only wear on Sunday. The worst part was that the girl he had saved from being forced to marry a guy with an ugly moustache and lousy taste in horses showed up, too. She stood around "gawking" at him with that awful, moonstruck look that always declared that there were no more fun parts coming. It was depressing.

Whether it was a movie I loved, or a great book I was reading, the endings were always hard for me, even the happy ones. I always wanted more. It seemed unfair to me. To be invited into their world and offered an intimate place in their lives for a while and then to be totally cut out and left with no recourse felt almost cruel. I didn't want them to leave. I wanted to share their next adventure, to laugh with them again, weep with them again, love with them again. I wanted my faithful allegiance to be rewarded with a permanent place in their world, but that was impossible now, because the last word had been written, the last scene had already faded to black.

I wonder if there wasn't a similar feeling for those who had been invited to share Jesus' life here on earth. They had become part of His world, laughed with Him, cried with Him, loved with Him, and dreamed about their future with Him; and then He was gone, and their last scene had faded to black. Maybe they felt cut out. Maybe it felt cruel to them. Maybe they were expecting that their faithful allegiance would be rewarded with a permanent place in His world. But now He was gone, and it was over—close the book, head for the exit, nothing else to see.

Jesus knew the ending would be hard for them, but He made them a promise. In light of His imminent departure, He said, *Therefore you now have sorrow; but I will see you again and your heart will rejoice, and your joy no one will take from you* (John 16:22). They would soon see that promise fulfilled and discover something their hearts always longed for—a story that never ends.

When Jesus walked out of the tomb that first Easter morning, He invited all of us to be an intimate and integral part of the greatest epic adventure the world would ever know, the greatest love story ever conceived, and the greatest mystery ever imagined—

and there would be no final scene, no last sentence, no closed book. Jesus didn't come just to give us a story to tell. He is the story. Like Him, it goes on forever, and He invites us to live it with Him.

In a world that seems devoted to turning life "upside down," living it with the One who created it is a major step toward turning things "right side up" again. The prayer that attends the closing pages of this book is that this little collection of vignettes will in some way draw every reader toward Him. My hope is that every one of us will be more deeply and intimately involved in the endless adventure that life with Him is, that we will look more carefully for examples of that love story every heart longs to experience, and that we'll find endless stimulation in the mysteries He unfolds all around us. Thank you for allowing me to share my heart with you on these pages.

Living in His Matchless Grace,
Ron Gallagher, Ed.S.

Meet the Author

RON GALLAGHER, Ed.S ~
Author, Speaker, Bible Teacher, Humorist, Satirist, Blogger
Looking at the World through the Lens of Biblical Truth

In addition to publishing *Gallagher's Pen*, a weekly blog addressing culturally relevant topics from a Biblical perspective, and contributing regularly to *Refresh Bible Study Magazine* and various freelance efforts, Ron is a church consultant, featured speaker, and newspaper columnist, none of which would have been found among his ambitions earlier in his life. His grandmother had great hopes that he would go into medicine, but by the time he reached his teens, he realized that the math requirements alone would never allow that dream to survive. From as early as the fourth grade, Ron had considered math to be nothing more than an evil conspiracy designed to torture children and render them incapable of future happiness. A career in jurisprudence, he decided, seemed to have so much more to offer—nice salary, not nearly as much exposure to internal organs, and clients could be examined without having to wear those embarrassing robes.

In spite of its appeal, Ron never made it to law school. Like multitudes of others with faded hopes and dreams, "life got in the way" for him, too. Education was expensive, and simply providing for life's necessities proved to be enough of a challenge. Funding a dream beyond that seemed unreachable. Then God invaded his life and implanted a different concept of who he was, why he was here, how he saw the world, and the direction his future should take.

Ron began to develop a passion for God's truth that eventually led him to surrender his life to ministry, but the path to that goal was not an easy one either. Education was still expensive, and balancing work and school was challenging. He began his academic journey as a Bible institute student, but later transferred to Liberty University, where he says that through hard work and dedication, he was able to "blaze" through a four-year degree program in only six years. But he quickly returns to a serious note and is careful to credit everything to the One who called him to Himself, redeemed his life, and provided what he needed when he needed it. That enabled him to continue on to a subsequent M.A. from Liberty Baptist Seminary and later, to earn an Ed.S degree in Counseling from The College of William and Mary.

Ron didn't suspect in those early days that his desire to share God's truth would eventually lead him to places like rural Alaska, where he and his wife lived in sight of an active volcano and worked together to lead a ministry to native Alaskans. In their free time, they engaged in things like harvesting king crabs, flying in bush planes, leading Bible conferences, panning for gold in the Yukon territory, and fishing within a few yards of whales and sea lions. Other than things like that, he says Alaska was pretty "dull."

Wherever Ron's ministry journey has led, he has been driven by a deep desire to be a source of help and encouragement to those struggling to find their way, and writing has always played a role in that effort. Whether preaching, teaching, consulting with church leaders, fighting to meet a writing deadline, or even working on a house-flipping project, Ron has sought to be a stabilizing voice with a *right side up* point of view in a world that so often seems turned *upside down*. Connect with him at www.gallagherspen.com or at GALLAGHERSPEN on both Facebook and Twitter.